Poems for Building Reading Skills

Camping

Sleeping in my sleeping bag
Here inside the tent,
Softly now the night breeze blows,
Through a netted vent.
Listening to the crickets sing
A joyful all-night tune,
Twinkling stars fill up the sky
Lit brightly by the moon.

Authors

Timothy Rasinski, Ph.D., and Karen McGuigan Brothers

Contributing Author

Beth Bray, M.S.

SHELL EDUCATION

Publishing Credits

Dona Herweck Rice, *Editor-in-Chief*; Lee Aucoin, *Creative Director*; Don Tran, *Print Production Manager;* Timothy J. Bradley, *Illustration Manager;* Conni Medina, M.S.Ed., *Editorial Director*; Evelyn Garcia, *Associate Editor*; Robin Erickson, *Interior Layout Designer;* Kelly Brownlee, Illustrator; Corinne Burton, M.S.Ed., *Publisher*

McREL Standards © 2004 www.mcrel.org/standards-benchmarks

All recordings performed by Holly Eiholzer. Recorded, edited, and mastered by Scott Zschomler at Lunar Studios.

Shell Education

5301 Oceanus Drive
Huntington Beach, CA 92649-1030
http://www.shelleducation.com
ISBN 978-1-4258-0677-4
© 2010 Shell Educational Publishing, Inc.

Table of Contents

Developing students' reading skills is a critical skill that begins in the primary grades. As you use the poems, lessons, and activities in this book, you will not only be providing instruction based on solid educational research, but also giving students opportunities to learn and practice specific academic standards.

The Poet and the Professor: Poems for Building Reading Skills is designed to provide high-interest instructional texts and lessons based on best practices in reading education. Each poem has an accompanying lesson plan with ideas for phonemic awareness, phonics, vocabulary, fluency, and comprehension activities based on the poem.

In an effort to identify the best practices in reading instruction, the National Reading Panel (2000) reviewed thousands of studies to determine key elements of effective reading instruction. The five essential areas of reading instruction are: phonemic awareness, phonics, vocabulary, fluency, and comprehension. The lessons in this book reflect these five elements of reading instruction.

Phonemic Awareness

Phonemic awareness refers to the awareness of the sounds of language and how language sounds work together to create words. Research shows that phonemic awareness is an excellent predictor of a student's future reading success (Adams 1990; Stanovich 1986; Yopp 1988). Although many students develop phonemic awareness informally, evidence suggests that phonemic awareness can be developed through direct instruction (Ball and Blachman 1991). Activities such as identifying, isolating, and categorizing phonemes, blending sounds to make words, segmenting sounds in words, and adding, deleting, and substituting phonemes require students to manipulate sounds in order to gain a better understanding of words (Yopp 1992; National Reading Panel 2000).

Each lesson in *The Poet and the Professor: Poems for Building Reading Skills* provides a phonemic awareness activity to train students in this important reading skill. Using words from the poem as a springboard, students are asked to manipulate phonemes. Although most of the phonemic awareness tasks are presented orally, there are also numerous activity pages that support phonemic awareness concepts. (See the Activity Skill—Correlation Chart on page 14.)

Phonics

During phonics instruction, students connect language sounds with corresponding written letters to see how they work together to form words that can be both read and written. Based on its review of studies, the National Reading Panel reports that explicit and systematic phonics instruction is an effective way to help students gain and apply knowledge of letter/sound relationships. The poems and activities in this book provide explicit ways to teach and reinforce phonics concepts appropriate to the primary grades.

The activities and teaching suggestions provided in each lesson are designed to help students improve word recognition and spelling skills. The activities focus on words or spelling patterns found in the poems.

Vocabulary

Our vocabulary consists of the words we know and use. These words help us communicate both verbally and in writing and also assist in reading comprehension. Vocabulary instruction can have direct effects on reading comprehension (Pressley 2002). Students who understand the words they read are more likely to comprehend the texts they read.

Students expand their vocabularies in many different ways. During direct word instruction, definitions are provided, as well as modeling and practice for using specific words in meaningful ways. Providing students with as few as two direct instructional strategies, allows them to understand the word when encountering it within a text (Baker, Simmons, and Kameenui 1998). The goal is to make students comfortable using new words in their own oral and written vocabularies through multiple, meaningful encounters with those words.

The vocabulary section of each lesson provides strategies and ideas for direct, meaningful instruction of words used in the poems. Words or phrases that may be unfamiliar or challenging to students have been selected from the poems for instruction. Students may be more familiar with some words than others. The purpose of this section is to provide in-depth instruction for words in the poems, thereby teaching meanings of new words and deepening understanding of those the student knows.

Fluency

Fluency refers to a student's ability to read accurately, effortlessly, and with expression (Rasinski 2003). Fluency instruction is important because fluent readers are better able to focus their attention on comprehension. Readers have a limited amount of attention to expend for reading. Students who use too much attention on word decoding understand less of what they read because they do not sufficiently focus attention on gaining meaning from the text (LaBerge and Samuels 1974).

One method of helping students gain fluency is repeated readings of a text. Studies on repeated readings have shown many benefits for readers. Students increase their comprehension as they group words in text into meaningful segments marked by expressive reading (O'Shea and Sindelar 1983). This method also helps students remember important information from a passage, including vocabulary (Bromage and Mayer 1986). Fluency rates and accurate word recognition can increase as students read other passages of equal or greater difficulty after mastering the original passage (Samuels 1979).

Providing meaningful and fun ways for students to return to a text can be a challenge. Poems are ideal texts for reading, rereading, and performing. The fluency section of each lesson and the corresponding activity pages give suggestions for students to reread the poems in fun, meaningful, and authentic ways that will provide the benefits that research shows for repeated readings.

Comprehension

We read for many different reasons—to learn something new, to enjoy a story, and to experience language are a few examples. Effective reading instruction must include teaching strategies that students can use to increase comprehension. Expert readers freely and appropriately use a variety of strategies to gain understanding as they read. Students need to effectively monitor their reading to maintain understanding and realize when their understanding has collapsed (Hosenfeld 1993). There are many effective strategies that teachers can use with students to assist with reading comprehension. These include using graphic organizers (Jensen 1998), predicting, rephrasing, answering questions, and generating questions (Bottomley and Osborn 1993). Teaching and modeling reading comprehension strategies through structured and explicit instruction enables students to learn how to comprehend text (Rosenshine and Meister 1994). The result of both explicit teaching and modeling is that students learn when and how to use these strategies to construct meaning (Carter 1997).

The comprehension section of each lesson provides strategies to help students increase their understanding of the poems. The suggestions vary from lesson to lesson, but include questions to ask students, discussion ideas, ways for students to demonstrate their understanding of the poem, and ideas for helping students make text-to-self and text-to-life connections. Many of the ideas and strategies can be used with any of the poems. Consider adapting your favorite comprehension ideas or strategies to other poems.

Word Study Extension

In a survey of words, Edward Fry (1998) found that by adding a consonant to the beginning of 38 rimes (the vowel plus the remaining consonants in a word, e.g., *ed, it, op*), more than 600 words can be read. This is a staggering and powerful number of words for a beginning reader to know. By studying and analyzing spelling patterns, students practice consolidating larger units of words or letter patterns that can then be applied to reading other words (Gaskins et al. 1997). Gaskins states, "Knowing consolidated units makes it easier to read and remember multisyllabic words as sight words, for it enables readers to deal with chunks of letters rather than each individual letter." The goal of teaching students to work with spelling patterns is to provide them with strategies for decoding words rapidly to increase fluency and comprehension.

A Word Study page is provided for each poem. First, students identify and categorize words from the poem and then build on that knowledge to create and categorize new words based on targeted rimes. For the second activity, students contextualize words by completing cloze sentences.

Using the poems, lessons, and activity pages in *The Poet and the Professor: Poems for Building Reading Skills* will provide a research-based and engaging way to teach elements essential to any reading program. By studying the poems in this book, students will practice and gain important strategies that will develop and strengthen their reading skills. Happy poetry reading!

Differentiation

Classrooms have evolved into diverse pools of learners including gifted students, English language learners, high achievers, learning-disabled students, underachievers, and average achievers. Teachers are expected to meet these diverse needs in one classroom. Differentiation encompasses what is taught, how it is taught, and the products students create to show what they have learned. These categories are often referred to as content, process, and product:

- Differentiating by content means putting more depth into the curriculum by organizing the curriculum concepts and structure of knowledge.
- Differentiating by process requires the use of varied instructional techniques and materials to enhance learning.
- Differentiating by product means that children are asked to show their learning in ways that will enhance their cognitive development and personal expression.

Teachers can keep these categories in mind as they plan instruction that will best meet the needs of their students.

Differentiating for Below-Grade-Level Students

Below-grade-level students will need concepts made more concrete for them. They may also need extra guidance in developing oral and written language. By receiving extra support and understanding, these students will feel more secure and have greater success. Suggested ideas include:

- Allow partner work for instructional activities.
- Allocate extra practice time.
- Allow for kinesthetic (hands-on) activities where appropriate.

Differentiating for Above-Grade-Level Students

These students usually learn concepts very quickly. The activities and end products can be adapted to be appropriate for individual students. Suggested ideas include:

- Assign students the activities that represent more complex concepts.
- Assign more complex oral and written responses.
- Have students design their own learning strategies and share them with the class.

Differentiating for English Language Learners

English language learners are an ever-increasing percentage of our school-age population. Like all students, English language learners need teachers who have a strong knowledge base and commitment to developing students' language. It is crucial that teachers work carefully to develop English language learners' academic vocabularies. Teachers should incorporate the following important practices:

- Create a comfortable atmosphere that encourages students to use language.
- Respect and draw on students' backgrounds and experiences and build connections between the known and the new.
- Model and scaffold language use.
- Make use of realia, concrete materials, visuals, pantomime, and other nonlinguistic representations of concepts to make input comprehensible. Write new words on the board as they are shared or provide each student with a set of cards that contain the words.
- Provide wait time to allow students the opportunity to gather their thoughts.

Differentiating by Proficiency Levels for English Language Learners

All teachers should know the levels of language acquisition for each of their English language learners. Knowing these levels will help to plan instruction. (The category titles vary from district to district or state to state, but the general descriptions are common.) Students at level 1 will need a lot of language support in all the activities. Using visuals to support oral and written language will help to make the language more comprehensible. These students "often understand much more than they are able to express" (Herrell and Jordan 2004). It is the teacher's job to move them from listening to language to expressing language. Students at levels 2 and 3 will benefit from pair work in speaking tasks, but they will need additional individual support during writing and reading tasks. Students at levels 4 and 5 (or 6, in some cases) may appear to be fully proficient in the English language. However, because they are English language learners, they may still struggle with comprehending the academic language used during instruction. They may also struggle with reading and writing.

The following chart shows the proficiency levels at a quick glance. The levels are based on the World-Class Instructional Design and Assessment (WIDA) Consortium (WIDA 2007).

Proficiency Levels at a Quick Glance

Proficiency Level	Questions to Ask	Activities/Actions		
Level 1—Entering minimal comprehension no verbal production	Where is…? What examples do you see? What are the parts of…?	listen point	draw circle	mime respond (one or two words)
Level 2—Beginning limited comprehension short spoken phrases	Can you list three…? What facts or ideas show…? What do the facts mean?	move match	select choose	act/act out list
Level 3—Developing increased comprehension simple sentences	How did ____ happen? Why do you think…? If you could __, what would you do?	name label	list categorize	respond (phrases or sentences) tell/say
Level 4—Expanding very good comprehension some errors in speech	How would you show…? What would result if…? Why is this important?	recall compare/contrast describe	retell explain role-play	define summarize restate
Level 5—Bridging comprehension comparable to native-English speakers speaks using complex sentences	What is meant by…? What is an original way to show…? Why is it better that…?	analyze evaluate create	defend justify describe	complete support express

How to Use This Book

The Poet and the Professor: Poems for Building Reading Skills is a succession of lessons built around a compilation of poems. The program includes this book (which is a teacher's resource for using the poems to build reading skills), the Audio CD, and the Teacher Resource CD.

This book features 30 original poems. Accompanying each poem is a lesson plan that contains the sections Phonemic Awareness, Phonics, Vocabulary, Fluency, Comprehension, and Word Study Extension. Information and ideas about how to relate the poem to each of these areas is provided on this page. For more information about each section, see the Research section of this book (pp. 4–6). In addition, two activity pages are provided that correspond to selected sections of the lesson plan.

The Audio CD contains recordings of each of the poems in the book. Students can follow the text on their own copies of the poem pages, on an interactive whiteboard, or on an overhead projector.

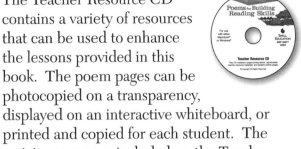

The Teacher Resource CD contains a variety of resources that can be used to enhance the lessons provided in this book. The poem pages can be photocopied on a transparency, displayed on an interactive whiteboard, or printed and copied for each student. The activity pages are included on the Teacher Resource CD. Finally, provided on the CD is a page-turning ebook that includes all of the poems used in this book. This page-turning ebook allows students to refer to all the poems in a digital format and can be displayed on an interactive whiteboard for easy viewing during a whole-class lesson.

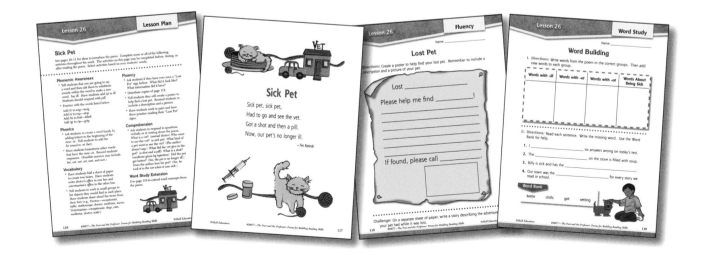

The Poet and the Professor: Poems for Building Reading Skills has been designed to supplement any reading language arts program. The following is a suggested routine for incorporating the poetry, reading comprehension, standards based skills, and word study activities into your weekly lessons.

Day	Suggested Instructional Plan
Day 1	• Display the poem. Provide a copy of the poem to each student. Read the poem with an expressive voice. Point to the words as you read the poem. • Read the poem several more times, inviting students to join in as they feel comfortable doing so. The goal is for students to become so familiar with the poem that they can read it on their own. • Briefly discuss the meaning of the poem and any outstanding literary features that you can point out to students (e.g., alliteration, rhymes). • Select an activity from the lesson page to do with students. The phonemic awareness activity is an excellent choice for the first day because it relates to words from the poem, but it does not require students to have extensive knowledge of the poem.
Day 2	• Reread the poem to students as they follow along silently or in a whisper voice. Be sure to point to the words as they are read. Read the poem chorally with students several times. • Select an activity or two from the lesson page to do with students. Expand on phonics vocabulary, fluency, or comprehension concepts from the poem. • Have each student dictate a brief personal response to the poem. Write students' responses on the board or a sheet of chart paper. Read the responses with students several times over the next few days.
Day 3	• Read the poem chorally once or twice with students. Have students try reading the poem on their own or with a partner. Ask students to read the poem several times, pointing to the words as they read. Observe students and provide encouragement as they read on their own. • Select an activity or two from the lesson page to do with students. Expand on phonics, vocabulary, fluency, or comprehension concepts from the poem. Provide students with the accompanying activity page if applicable.

Day	Suggested Instructional Plan
Day 4	• Pair students again (or have them work in trios or quartets) and have them read the poem to each other. Or refer to the Fluency section of the lesson plan for additional ideas for reading the poem. • Distribute copies of the Word Study activity sheet. Focus on the rimes or word families from the poem that have been selected for this activity. In the chart, show students the word part, and write words that can be made from the word families. Once students write the words, have them practice reading them. • Have students use the words from the Word Building activity to complete the sentences activity. Have students try to read the sentences. If they are not yet able to do so, read the sentences with them. Students should then choose the correct word that goes in the appropriate blank. A Word Bank is provided to assist students with this section.
Day 5	• Have students read the poem to you, individually or as a group. After several poems have been covered, allow students to choose poems from previous weeks to perform for the class. Complete any other activities from the lesson plan that you wish to do with students. • Have students refer to the Word Study activity sheet they have completed. Create a list of all the word family words that students created in the Word Building activity. Write each word on a 3" x 5" index card. Place the cards in a pocket chart. Have students practice reading the words. • Rearrange the word cards so that students focus their attention on the words and are not reading them from practice and memory. Also, feel free to add words from previous lessons for this activity. • Sort the words into various piles by their sounds—at the beginning, middle, or end of the words. For example, find all words that begin with the /b/ sound and put them in one pile. • Play word games, such as Memory. Make a duplicate set of word cards, turn both sets over, and have students try to match them, saying the words as they turn them over. • Above all, have fun with the poems. Help students find enjoyment in the rhyme, expression, and cadence found in reading rhythmical words aloud.

Standards Correlations

Shell Education is committed to producing educational materials that are research- and standards-based. In this effort, we have correlated all of our products to the academic standards of all 50 states, the District of Columbia, and the Department of Defense Dependent Schools.

How to Find Standards Correlations

To print a customized correlation report of this product for your state, visit our website at **www.shelleducation.com** and follow the on-screen directions. If you require assistance in printing correlation reports, please contact Customer Service at 1-877-777-3450.

Purpose and Intent of Standards

The No Child Left Behind legislation mandates that all states adopt academic standards that identify the skills students will learn in kindergarten through grade twelve. While many states had already adopted academic standards prior to NCLB, the legislation set requirements to ensure the standards were detailed and comprehensive.

Standards are designed to focus instruction and guide adoption of curricula. Standards are statements that describe the criteria necessary for students to meet specific academic goals. They define the knowledge, skills, and content students should acquire at each level. Standards are also used to develop standardized tests to evaluate students' academic progress.

Teachers are required to demonstrate how their lessons meet state standards. State standards are used in development of all of our products, so educators can be assured they meet the academic requirements of each state.

McREL Compendium

Shell Education uses the Mid-continent Research for Education and Learning (McREL) Compendium to create standards correlations. Each year, McREL analyzes state standards and revises the compendium. By following this procedure, McREL is able to produce a general compilation of national standards. Each lesson in this product is based on one or more McREL standards. The chart on the following pages list each standard taught in this product and the page numbers of the corresponding lessons.

Standards Correlation Chart

The chart below correlates the activities in *The Poet and the Professor: Poems for Building Reading Skills* with the McREL Content Knowledge.

Standards for Language Arts Grades 3–5

Standards	Benchmarks	Lesson
Uses the general skills and strategies of the writing process	1.6 Uses strategies to write for a variety of purposes	4, 14, 25, 27, 30
	1.11 Writes in response to literature	3, 4, 13, 27, 30
Uses the stylistic and rhetorical aspects of writing	2.1 Uses descriptive language that clarifies and enhances	6, 14, 27, 30
	2.3 Uses a variety of sentence structures in writing	14, 25, 27, 30
Uses the general skills and strategies of the reading process	5.4 Uses basic elements of phonetic analysis to decode unknown words	All
	5.7 Understands level-appropriate sight words and vocabulary	6, 11, 16, 22
	5.8 Reads aloud familiar stories, poems, and passages with fluency and expression	All
Uses reading skills and strategies to understand and interpret a variety of literary texts	6.1 Uses reading skills and strategies to understand a variety of familiar literary passages and texts	2, 5, 7, 18, 28
Uses listening and speaking skills for different purposes	8.1 Makes contributions in class and group discussions	All
	8.2 Asks and responds to questions	1, 7, 8, 10, 12, 14, 19, 26, 28
	8.5 Uses level-appropriate vocabulary in speech	3, 4, 7, 9, 10, 13, 15, 17, 20, 21, 23, 24, 29
	8.7 Recites and responds to familiar stories, poems, and rhymes with patterns	5, 12, 22

Activity Skill—Correlation Chart

McREL Content Knowledge Standards for Language Arts Grades 3–5

Activity Page	Standards-Based Skill or Focus	Page
Phonemic Awareness		
Doesn't Belong	Phoneme Categorization	18
Happy Halloween	Phoneme Categorization	38
Digraphs	Phoneme Identity	50
Listen Up	Phoneme Identity	86
Make New Words	Phoneme Addition & Subtraction	106
Phonics		
Cow Bow	Spelling Pattern (-ow)	34
Word Families	Spelling Patterns (-op and -out)	54
Blends	Words with Blends	66
Telephone Endings	Word Endings	70
EE Puzzle	Spelling pattern -ee	74
Final *e*	Spelling Pattern (Long Vowels)	114
Silly Sounds	Initial Consonants	126
Vocabulary		
Going to the Circus	Categorization	46
Farm Animals	Word Clues	78
Blast Off	Antonyms	82
Nighttime	Categorization	90
Describing Words	Adjectives and Nouns	94
Homophones	Homophones	130
Flying Machines	Word Identification	134
Fluency		
Partner Reading	High Frequency	22
Write Your Own Poem	High Frequency	26
Reader's Theater	High Frequency	30
Poem Book	High Frequency	98
Say It Well	Phrasing	110
Lost Pet	High Frequency	118
Reader's Theater	High Frequency	122
Comprehension		
Right There Questions	Responding to Questions	42
Winter Words	Vocabulary to Aid Comprehension	58
My Birthday	Text-to-Life Connection	62
Looking Back and More	Responding to Questions	102

About the Poets

Dr. Timothy Rasinski, Ph.D, is a Professor of Education in the Reading and Writing Center at Kent State University, Ohio, where he directs the reading clinic. His scholarly interests include reading fluency, word study, reading in the elementary and middle grades, and readers who struggle. He has served on the Board of Directors of the International Reading Association and is widely published in reading journals. His book *The Fluent Reader* provides background information and practical applications for the teaching of fluency. Dr. Rasinski speaks all over the country to education audiences about reading fluency. His research on fluency has been cited by the National Reading Panel and was influential in having fluency included as one of the five essential components of reading instruction in the Reading First legislation.

Karen McGuigan Brothers recently retired from the Reading and Writing Development Center at Kent State University, Kent, Ohio. For nearly 30 years, she served as the liaison for parents and teachers inquiring about participation in the Center's testing and tutoring programs in reading and also coordinated the development of those programs. Through exposure to children's literature at the Center, as well as her experience as a mother and grandmother, she became familiar with what subject matter appeals to children and incorporates that into her poetry. In addition to co-authoring *The Poet and the Professor: Poems for Building Reading Skills*, she has written children's poems for numerous other publications.

Home Alone

See pages 10–11 for ideas to introduce the poem. Complete some or all of the following activities throughout the week. The activities on this page may be completed before, during, or after reading the poem. Select activities based on your students' needs.

Phonemic Awareness

- Distribute copies of page 18.
- Ask students to mark an *X* on the picture in each row that does not have the same middle sound as the other two pictures.

Phonics

- Write the words *like* and *bike* on the board or on a sheet of chart paper. Point to the *-ike* spelling pattern in both words.
- Ask students to create new words by writing different letters and blends in front of the *-ike* spelling pattern. Encourage students to create real words and nonsense words. Write students' responses.

Vocabulary

- Develop students' knowledge of various types of homes by discussing other names for homes. Ask students to brainstorm other names for homes (e.g., *house, apartment, condominium, townhouse, mobile home*). Write students' responses on the board or on a sheet of chart paper.
- Ask students questions regarding particular homes. *Who lives in an igloo?* (Eskimo) *Who lives in a longhouse?* (American Indians) *A tent is an ideal home for who?* (Nomad)
- Tell students to complete the cloze sentences below:

   _____ lives in a _____.

   _____ I live in a _____.

Fluency

- Ask students to use a red crayon and circle all the words in the poem that rhyme with *alone*. Ask students where these words appear in the poem (at the end of each line).
- Tell students that they will read the poem aloud, pausing after the rhyming words no matter how the sentence is punctuated. Have students choral-read together, pausing and reading with expression.

Comprehension

- Ask students whether they have ever been home alone. What did they do? If not, have them imagine that they were home alone. What would they do? Brainstorm ideas and write them on the board or on a sheet of chart paper.
- Ask students to write three things they would do if they were home alone.

Word Study Extension

Use page 19 to extend word concepts from the poem.

Home Alone

When you're home alone,

You can use the phone,

Give your dog a bone,

Eat an ice cream cone,

Or sit there like a stone—

When you're home alone.

—Karen McGuigan Brothers

Name: _____

Doesn't Belong

Directions: *Look at the pictures in each row. Say each word aloud. Make an X over the picture that does not have the same middle sound as the other two pictures.*

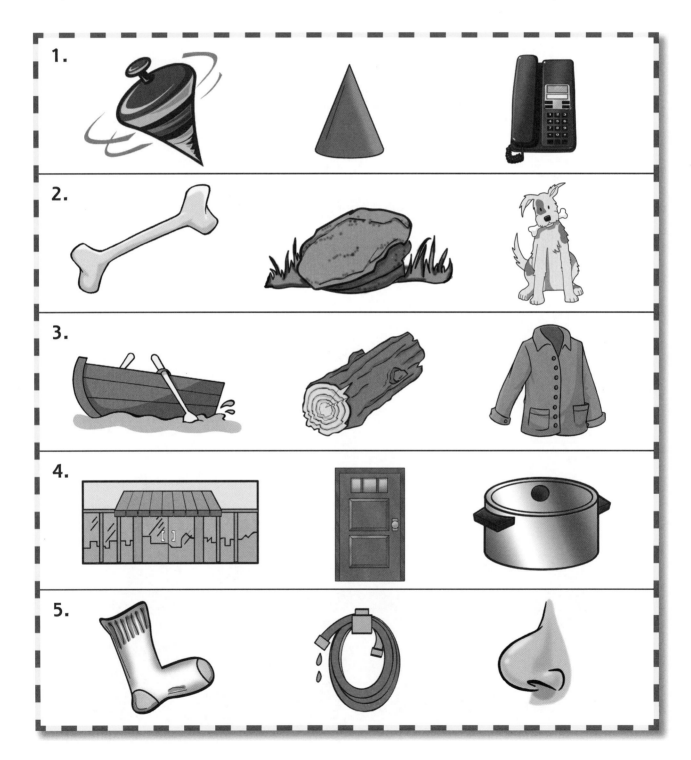

Name: _____

Word Building

I. Directions: *Write words from the poem in the correct groups. Then add new words to each group.*

Words with *-one*	Words with *-ome*	Words with *-ice*	Words About Being Alone

• •

II. Directions: *Read each sentence. Write the missing word. Use the Word Bank for help.*

1. *I talk to my friend on the _____ every day.*

2. *Our bodies are made of skin and _____.*

3. *My _____ has three bedrooms.*

4. *My teacher is very _____.*

Word Bank

phone   bones   nice   home

The Drain

See pages 10–11 for ideas to introduce the poem. Complete some or all of the following activities throughout the week. The activities on this page may be completed before, during, or after reading the poem. Select activities based on your students' needs.

Phonemic Awareness

- Tell students that you will say a word and then ask them to change the beginning sound or ending sound in order to make a new word. Say the word *pick*. Have students change the /p/ in *pick* to /s/. Students should respond with *sick*.

- Practice with the words listed below:

  Change the /d/ in *drain* to /t/—*train*

  Change the /tr/ in *train* to /p/—*pain*

  Change the /n/ in *pain* to /r/—*pair*

Phonics

- Ask students to circle the words *drink* and *drain* in the poem. Explain that both words begin with the *dr-* spelling pattern.

- Have students work in groups of four to brainstorm and record words that begin with the *dr-* spelling pattern.

- Ask each group to read their words to the class. Record all the words on the board or on a sheet of chart paper. As words are repeated, circle the words that are the same on more than one list.

Vocabulary

- Ask students to identify the words in the poem that end in *-ed* (*used, leaned, sucked*). Explain that adding *-ed* to the end of a verb tells the reader that the action happened in the past.

- Have students brainstorm other past tense verbs with *-ed*. Write students' responses on the board or on a sheet of chart paper.

Fluency

- Distribute copies of page 22.

- Tell students to use a blue crayon to circle the words that end in *-ink*. Tell students to use a red crayon to circle the words that end in *-ain*.

- Ask students to partner-read the poem to practice fluency.

Comprehension

- In the poem, the author writes, "…*if I leaned in to get a drink*…" Ask students to think about what the author is leaning into. On the board or on a sheet of chart paper, write students' responses that make sense in the context of the poem.

- Reread the poem with these ideas in mind. Tell students to draw a picture of what they think the author means.

Word Study Extension

Use page 23 to extend word concepts from the poem.

The Drain

When I was young

I used to think,

If I leaned in

To get a drink,

I'd be sucked

Into the drain,

Just like water

After rain.

—Karen McGuigan Brothers

Name: _____

Partner Reading

Directions: Use a blue crayon to circle the words that end in -ink. Use a red crayon to circle the words that end in -ain. Partner-read with another classmate. Read together alternating lines, and then switch lines. Finally, read the whole poem together again.

The Drain

When I was young

I used to think,

If I leaned in

To get a drink,

I'd be sucked

Into the drain,

Just like water

After rain.

—Karen McGuigan Brothers

Name: _____

Word Building

I. Directions: *Write words from the poem in the correct groups. Then add new words to each group.*

Words with -*ink*	Words with -*ain*	Words with -*et*	Words About Rain

II. Directions: *Read each sentence. Write the missing word. Use the Word Bank for help.*

1. *I hope my toy doesn't* _____ *in the pool.*

2. *When did you* _____ *home?*

3. *The baseball game was delayed because of the* _____ .

4. *Don't* _____ *too much soda pop.*

Word Bank

sink   get   rain   drink

My Scooter

See pages 10–11 for ideas to introduce the poem. Complete some or all of the following activities throughout the week. The activities on this page may be completed before, during, or after reading the poem. Select activities based on your students' needs.

Phonemic Awareness

- Tell students that they will break words into separate sounds. Say the word *park*. Ask students how many sounds they hear in *park*. Students should respond /p/, /ar/, /k/ (three).

- Explain that the word *park* has four letters, but only three sounds can be heard because the letters *a* and *r* work together.

- Continue with the words below:

    dark—/d/, /ar/, /k/ (three)

    mark—/m/, /ar/, /k/ (three)

Phonics

- Ask students to create a word family by adding letters to the beginning of the rime *-ark*. Tell students to add the /b/ sound to *-ark*. Students should respond with *bark*.

- Continue with the following sounds:

    Add /d/ to *-ark*—*dark*

    Add /m/ to *-ark*—*mark*

Vocabulary

- Tell students that they will investigate words that are spelled the same, but have different meanings. In the poem, the author uses the word *park*. Discuss the multiple meanings of the word *park* (e.g., playing at a nearby park, parking a car).

- Distribute sheets of paper and have students fold the paper vertically. In the left column, ask students to write and leave space between the following words: *park, cold, play, can,* and *left*.

- Tell students to use each word in two sentences that use the two meanings. Sentences should be written in the right column. For example:

    I went to the *park*.

    Park the car in the garage.

Fluency

- Distribute copies of page 26.

- Tell students that they will write their own poems using the sentence frames provided. Tell students that they may select words from the Word Bank if they wish. Ask students to share their poems with three classmates.

Comprehension

- Tell students to look at the poem and identify the sequence of events.

- Distribute sheets of paper and ask students to fold their paper to make three columns. At the top of each column, ask students to write *beginning, middle,* and *end*.

- Ask students to write a sentence or two and draw a picture to represent the events of the poem.

Word Study Extension

Use page 27 to extend word concepts from the poem.

My Scooter

I love to ride my scooter.

I ride it in the park.

I ride it on the sidewalk—

But never after dark.

—Karen McGuigan Brothers

Name: _____

Write Your Own Poem

Directions: *Read the sentences below. Choose a word from the Word Bank, or use your own words to finish the sentences. Share your poem with three classmates.*

My _____

I love to ride my _____ .

I ride it in the _____ .

I ride it on the _____ .

I ride it to the _____ .

I ride it with my _____ .

Word Bank

scooter	bike	skateboard	store	park	yard	house
sidewalk	street	playground	friend	school	brother	sister

Name: _____

Word Building

I. Directions: *Write words from the poem in the correct groups. Then add new words to each group.*

Words with **-ark**	Words with **-ide**	Words with **-oot**	Words About Scooters

II. Directions: *Read each sentence. Write the missing word. Use the Word Bank for help.*

1. *I like to play _____-and-seek.*

2. *When it is _____, I turn on the lights.*

3. *I heard the owl _____ last night.*

4. *I like to play on the _____ at the park.*

Word Bank

hide   hoot   slide   dark

Exercise

See pages 10–11 for ideas to introduce the poem. Complete some or all of the following activities throughout the week. The activities on this page may be completed before, during, or after reading the poem. Select activities based on your students' needs.

Phonemic Awareness

- Tell students that they will create a new word by deleting a sound from another word. Ask students to say the word *pride* without the /p/ sound. Students should respond *ride*.

- Repeat this with the following words:

  skid without /s/—*kid*

  stop without /s/—*top*

  play without /p/—*lay*

  snap without /s/—*nap*

Phonics

- Distribute sheets of paper and ask students to fold their papers vertically.

- Tell students that they will create word families with the rimes *-ike* and *-un*. Ask students to write the rime *-ike* at the top of one column and the rime *-un* at the top of the other column.

- Encourage students to make word families by adding beginning letters to each rime (e.g., *like, bike, hike, spike, sun, bun, fun*).

Vocabulary

- Review with students what an adjective is (a describing word). Say the phrase "old Uncle Jim." Ask students what the adjective is in the phrase. Students should respond with *old*.

- Tell students to add an adjective to their names, using alliteration if possible (e.g., *Beautiful Beth, Super Scott*). Have students share their adjectives.

Fluency

- Distribute copies of page 30.

- Put students into groups of four and assign parts. Have students practice reading their assigned parts with their groups. Once groups have practiced, ask each group to take turns in sharing their scripts with the class.

Comprehension

- Discuss with students the purpose of the poem (telling fun ways to exercise).

- Ask students to brainstorm other ways people exercise. Write students' responses on the board or on a sheet of chart paper.

- Tell students to select one of the activities listed and write a paragraph describing why they would exercise that way.

Word Study Extension

Use page 31 to extend word concepts from the poem.

Exercise

"Swim, swim! You'll like to swim,"
Says my dear old Uncle Jim.

"Bike, bike! Get on your bike,"
Says my active Uncle Mike.

"Don't mope! Just jump a rope,"
Says my jumpy Auntie Hope.

"Run, run! Play in the sun,"
I say myself. "Let's have some fun!"

—Tim Rasinski

Name: _____

Reader's Theater

Directions: *In groups of four, choose a part to read. Practice your lines. Read with expression, as if you are trying to convince a classmate to exercise. Practice the poem together, with each student reading his or her part.*

Student One: Swim, swim! You'll like to swim!

Student Two: Bike, bike! Get on your bike!

Student Three: Don't mope! Just jump a rope!

Student Four: Run, run! Play in the sun!

All Students: So do your exercise for fun. Swim and bike and jump and run!

Name: _____

Word Building

I. Directions: *Write words from the poem in the correct groups. Then add new words to each group.*

Words with **-un**	Words with **-ope**	Words with **-ike**	Words About Exercise

II. Directions: *Read each sentence. Write the missing word. Use the Word Bank for help.*

1. We can play outside when the _____ is out.

2. I _____ my wish comes true.

3. My brother Mike likes to ride his _____ .

4. When I am sad, I _____ around the house.

Word Bank

hope   mope
sun   bike

Twenty-Two Lions

See pages 10–11 for ideas to introduce the poem. Complete some or all of the following activities throughout the week. The activities on this page may be completed before, during, or after reading the poem. Select activities based on your students' needs.

Phonemic Awareness

- Tell students that they will create new words by substituting sounds. Say the word *mean*. Ask students to change the /n/ sound to a /t/ sound. Students should respond with *meat*.

- Continue with the following substitutions:

  Change /m/ in *meat* to /s/—*seat*

  Change /t/ in *seat* to /l/—*seal*

  Change /s/ in *seal* to /r/—*real*

Phonics

- Write the words *cow* and *grow* on the board or on a sheet of chart paper. Discuss how both words have the *-ow* spelling pattern, yet sound differently in each word. Ask students to brainstorm other words that have the *-ow* spelling pattern at the end of the word. Write students' responses on the board or on a sheet of chart paper.

- Distribute copies of page 34.

- Tell students that they will need to complete the sentences by correctly selecting words from the Word Bank that have the *-ow* spelling pattern.

Vocabulary

- Tell students to circle the words in the poem that end with *-in* (e.g., *lookin'*, *chowin'*). Ask students to identify the missing letter in each word. (The letter *g* is missing to make the *-ing* suffix.)

- Ask students to brainstorm verbs with the *-ing* suffix (e.g., *running*, *jumping*, *playing*, *singing*, *climbing*). Write students' responses on the board or on a sheet of chart paper.

Fluency

- Have students color-code the poem by alternating using a blue and red crayon to underline each line of the poem. Divide students into two groups. Have one group read the words underlined in red and the other group read the words underlined in blue.

- After students finish reading their lines, have them switch lines. Model intonation and phrasing during the readings.

Comprehension

- Discuss with students the tone or mood of the poem. Read the poem and ask students to look for words that help the reader determine the mood of the poem (e.g., *mean*, *frown-faced*).

- Ask students to rewrite the poem in a light and happy tone by selecting different words.

Word Study Extension

Use page 35 to extend word concepts from the poem.

Twenty-Two Lions

I went to the circus,
In a tent downtown.
There were twenty-two lions
And twenty-two clowns.
Mean lookin' lions
And frown-faced clowns,
'Cause the lions were chowin',
Chowin' on clowns.
Twenty-two lions, and—
Oops! Twenty-one clowns.

—Tim Rasinski

Name: _____

Cow Bow

Directions: Select the correct words from the Word Bank to complete the sentences. Notice that words that end the same can sound different.

1. The farmer uses a _____ in the fields.

2. Bridget ties a _____ in her hair.

3. Sam and Carlos _____ a boat on a trailer.

4. Can I have lunch _____?

5. Seeds _____ into plants.

6. The farmer milks the _____ every day.

Word Bank

bow tow cow
plow grow now

Challenge: On a separate sheet of paper, write a new sentence for each word in the Word Bank.

Name: _____

Word Building

I. Directions: *Write words from the poem in the correct groups. Then add new words to each group.*

Words with -*ent*	Words with -*own*	Words with -*oo*	Words About the Circus

• •

II. Directions: *Read each sentence. Write the missing word. Use the Word Bank for help.*

1. We went to _____ to buy books.

2. There was a big _____ on the side of the car.

3. I won't put the bait on the _____ .

4. Mom _____ my brother
to find my sister.

Word Bank

dent   town   hook   sent

Halloween

See pages 10–11 for ideas to introduce the poem. Complete some or all of the following activities throughout the week. The activities on this page may be completed before, during, or after reading the poem. Select activities based on your students' needs.

Phonemic Awareness

- Discuss with students the term *alliteration* (the repetition of consonant sounds in two or more words). Explain to students that the phrase "Spooky Scary Spiders" is an alliteration because the words start with the same sound.
- Distribute copies of page 38.
- Tell students they will be creating a Halloween poem using alliteration.

Phonics

- Ask students to find and circle the following blends from the poem: *bl, sp, fl,* and *sm.*
- Have students work in small groups to brainstorm words that begin with these blends. Write students' responses on the board or on a sheet of chart paper.

Vocabulary

- Ask students to name words associated with Halloween. Write students' responses on the board or on a sheet of chart paper.
- Distribute blank sheets of paper to students. Tell them to select eight Halloween words from the list and draw a picture to match the definition for each word.

Fluency

- Reread the poem in unison with students. Ask students to pay close attention to the sound of your voice. As you read the poem, change the volume of your voice from a whisper to a shout.
- Continue modeling the phrasing of the poem. Students will enjoy this activity, and you may want students to lead the class.

Comprehension

- Ask students to tell you in what season Halloween falls. Ask students to name other important days that are during the fall season. Write students' responses on the board or on a sheet of chart paper.
- Tell students to select one day listed on the board and write how they celebrate that day.

Word Study Extension

Use page 39 to extend word concepts from the poem.

Halloween

Howling cats and a big black spider,

Flying bats, some doughnuts and cider,

Smiling pumpkins can be seen;

The time is here for Halloween.

—Karen McGuigan Brothers

Name: _____

Happy Halloween

Directions: Use the words from the Word Bank to create a new Halloween poem. Choose words with the same beginning sounds for each line. When you are finished, read the poem to a classmate.

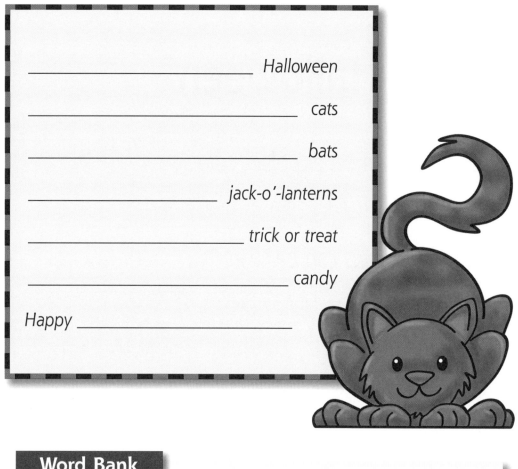

_____ Halloween

_____ cats

_____ bats

_____ jack-o'-lanterns

_____ trick or treat

_____ candy

Happy _____

Word Bank

Kids collecting   Creepy, crying   Jagged-jawed
Halloween   Big, black   Happy
Terrible twins

Challenge: On a separate sheet of paper, write a spooky story using the words from the Word Bank.

Name: _____

Word Building

I. Directions: Write words from the poem in the correct groups. Then add new words to each group.

Words with -*een*	Words with -*er*	Words with -*ack*	Words About Halloween

II. Directions: Read each sentence. Write the missing word. Use the Word Bank for help.

1. When I turn thirteen, I'll be a _____.

2. The _____ bee was protecting the workers.

3. People can make _____ from apples.

4. I have a _____ of library books.

Word Bank

cider   queen   teenager   stack

A Little Green Boy

See pages 10–11 for ideas to introduce the poem. Complete some or all of the following activities throughout the week. The activities on this page may be completed before, during, or after reading the poem. Select activities based on your students' needs.

Phonemic Awareness

- Tell students that you will say a sound and a word. Ask them to tell you the new word that is made when you add the sound to the beginning of the word. Tell students to add /g/ to *low*. Students should respond with *glow*.

- Continue with the words below:

  lay—add the /p/ sound—*play*

  out—add the /sh/ sound—*shout*

  ice—add the /r/ sound—*rice*

Phonics

- Ask students to name beginning sounds they hear in the word *spaceship*. Students should respond with the /s/ and /p/ sounds.

- Ask students to name other words that begin with the *sp-* spelling pattern (e.g., *spit*, *spin*, *speed*). Record students' responses.

Vocabulary

- Explain that the word *spaceship* is a *compound word* because it is made by putting two words together to form a new word. Ask students to name other compound words. Record students' answers.

- Tell students that you will say some words. If they can think of another word to add to create a compound word, they should raise their hands. Say the following words: *door*, *mail*, *stop*, *fire*, and *foot*. Record the compound words that students say.

Fluency

- Tell students to use a red crayon to underline the words in the poem that rhyme with *say*. Use these words to indicate a phrase mark or a place to pause when reading.

- Ask students to echo-read the poem in pairs. During echo-reading, one student echoes the other student, mimicking intonation and phrasing. After students complete the reading, have students switch roles.

Comprehension

- Tell students that a good strategy to remember what they just read, is to look back at the text.

- Distribute copies of page 42.

- Ask students to complete the activity by looking back at the poem to answer the questions.

Word Study Extension

Use page 43 to extend word concepts from the poem.

A Little Green Boy

A little green boy came from Mars one day.

He asked if I could come out to play.

We flew in his spaceship, up and away,

And traveled throughout the Milky Way.

—Karen McGuigan Brothers

Name: _____

Right There Questions

Directions: *Read the poem and answer the questions. Look back in the poem and underline the word or words that helped you find the answer. Use complete sentences in your answers.*

1. What color is the little boy? _____

_____

2. Where is the little boy from? _____

_____

3. What did the little boy ask? _____

_____

4. Where did the little boy go to play? _____

_____

5. Where do you think the Milky Way is? _____

_____

6. Use your imagination. What games would you choose to play with the little green boy?

_____

_____

Challenge: *Write a journal entry about your journey with the little green boy.*

Name: _____

Word Building

I. Directions: Write words from the poem in the correct groups. Then add new words to each group.

Words with -*ay*	Words with -*oy*	Words with -*out*	Words About Outer Space

II. Directions: Read each sentence. Write the missing word. Use the Word Bank for help.

1. When the ice cream truck comes, I _____, "Stop!"

2. My friends are _____ and _____.

3. When I get mad, I tend to _____.

4. One _____, I fell off my bike.

Word Bank

day   Floyd   shout   pout   Roy

The Circus

See pages 10–11 for ideas to introduce the poem. Complete some or all of the following activities throughout the week. The activities on this page may be completed before, during, or after reading the poem. Select activities based on your students' needs.

Phonemic Awareness

- Tell students that they will segment words by saying one sound at a time. Say the word *town* segmented into sounds: /t/, /ow/, /n/. Ask students to repeat the sounds in the word *town* and then write the word.

- Continue with the following words: *plus, bug, plug, dug,* and *smug*.

Phonics

- Ask students to say the word *circus*. Write the word *circus* on the board or on a sheet of chart paper. Tell students that the letter *c* can make two different sounds: /s/ or /k/.

- Tell students to fold a sheet of paper in half to make two columns. In one column, have students write *soft c words* /s/. In the other column, have students write *hard c words* /k/.

- Tell students to write words with the soft *c* (e.g., *circle, center*) in the appropriate column. Tell students to write words with the hard *c* (e.g., *car, comb*) in the appropriate column.

Vocabulary

- Distribute copies of page 46.

- Ask students to circle words from the poem that name people and animals. Tell students to classify the circus words as people or animals.

Fluency

- Ask students to read the first line of the poem. Ask them how the line would sound with a punctuation at the end.

- Encourage students to practice rereading these sentences with a different punctuation at the end of the sentence:

    I went to the circus?

    I went to the circus.

    I went to the circus!

Comprehension

- Ask students to identify the animals that are listed in this poem. Ask what animals they would have if they owned a circus. Why? What tricks would the animals do?

- Have students record their answers on a blank sheet of paper or in their journals. Encourage students to name their circus and include illustrations.

Word Study Extension

Use page 47 to extend word concepts from the poem.

The Circus

I went to the circus

When it came to town.

I saw striped tigers—

Orange and brown—

Some dancing ponies,

A funny-faced clown,

And a silly monkey

In a purple gown.

—Karen McGuigan Brothers

Name: _____

Going to the Circus

Directions: List people and animals you might find at a circus on the chart. Use the Word Bank to help you.

People	Animals

Word Bank

tigers   clowns   elephants   trapeze artist   monkeys
bears   ponies   lion-tamer   tightrope walker   acrobat

• •

Challenge: On a separate sheet of paper, write a newspaper article about an exciting event that happened at the circus. Use the words from the Word Bank to help you.

Name: _____

Word Building

I. Directions: *Write words from the poem in the correct groups. Then add new words to each group.*

Words with -own	Words with -ame	Words with -us	Words About Clowns

● ●

II. Directions: *Read each sentence. Write the missing word. Use the Word Bank for help.*

1. Six _____ four equals ten.

2. The lion was not _____ .

3. Mr. Smith is the mayor of my _____ .

4. If you fall _____ , get right back up.

Word Bank

down   town   plus   tame

Ants

See pages 10–11 for ideas to introduce the poem. Complete some or all of the following activities throughout the week. The activities on this page may be completed before, during, or after reading the poem. Select activities based on your students' needs.

Phonemic Awareness

- Discuss with students what a *digraph* is (a pair of letters that make a single sound). Say the word *quiet*. Tell students that the beginning digraph in *quiet* is *qu*.
- Ask students to identify the beginning digraph in the word *chin*. Students should respond /ch/.
- Distribute copies of page 50.
- Tell students to say the name of each picture and write the beginning digraph on the lines.

Phonics

- Ask students to brainstorm words that have the rime *-ant*. Many of the words will be nonsense words.
- Encourage students to categorize the words as real or nonsense as they verbally state the words. Help students get started by saying the word *ant*.

Vocabulary

- Read the poem. Have students circle the words *Battled* and *harmony* in the poem. Discuss with students the definition of the words in student-friendly language.
- Write the words *battled* and *harmony* on the board and ask students to name some synonyms for each word (e.g., *fought, argued, peace, unity*). Reread the poem, substituting the synonyms.

Fluency

- Have students work in pairs to practice reading the poem with a different role.
- Assign one student to read the narrator lines, and have the other student read the queen lines. After students complete the reading, have them switch roles.

Comprehension

- Discuss with students the differences between red and black ants. Ask students questions such as where they live, how many legs they have, how many body parts they have, what they eat, and how they move. Record students' responses on a Venn diagram.
- Ask students if they think ants should battle because they look different.

Word Study Extension

Use page 51 to extend word concepts from the poem.

Ants

The red and black ants

Battled hard one day,

'Til the red queen asked,

"Why fight in this way?

We both have our hills.

Let's find harmony!

For though our colors differ,

We're all ants, you see."

—Karen McGuigan Brothers

Name: _____

Digraphs

Directions: *Look at each picture. Say the word aloud. Use the Sound Bank to write the beginning digraph under each picture to match its beginning sound.*

1. 	2. 	3. 	4. 
_____	_____	_____	_____
5. 	6. 	7. **3**	8. 
_____	_____	_____	_____
9. 	10. 	11. 	12. 
_____	_____	_____	_____
13. **1,000**	14. 	15. 	16. 
_____	_____	_____	_____

Sound Bank

qu   sh   ch   th

Challenge: *Write three new words that begin with each digraph.*

Name: _____

Word Building

I. Directions: *Write words from the poem in the correct groups. Then add new words to each group.*

Words with -*ay*	Words with -*ant*	Words with -*ight*	Words About Friends

II. Directions: *Read each sentence. Write the missing word. Use the Word Bank for help.*

1. On vacations, I want to _____ in hotels.

2. The old deer had huge _____ .

3. Don't turn left, go _____ .

4. I tore my _____ when I fell.

Word Bank

stay   right   antlers   pants

Soda Pop

See pages 10–11 for ideas to introduce the poem. Complete some or all of the following activities throughout the week. The activities on this page may be completed before, during, or after reading the poem. Select activities based on your students' needs.

Phonemic Awareness

- Tell students that you will say some words, and they are to identify the medial sound in the words. Say the word *pop*. Ask students to say the vowel sound in the word *pop* (/ŏ/).

- Continue with other CVC (consonant-vowel-consonant) words listed below:

  pig—/ĭ /   *pun*—/ŭ/
  pen—/ĕ/   *pat*—/ă/

Phonics

- Tell students that they will create word families with the rimes *-op* and *-out*. Write the rimes *-op* and *-out* on the board or on a sheet of chart paper.

- Encourage students to name word families by adding beginning letters to each rime. Write students' responses under each corresponding rime.

- Distribute copies of page 54.

Vocabulary

- Ask students to reread the poem and identify people from the poem who help others (e.g., *nurse, cop*). Remind students that *nurse* and *cop* are *common nouns*. Explain that common nouns are general names for people, places, and things, while *proper nouns* are specific names of people, places, and things.

- Have students work in groups of four to brainstorm other common nouns for people who help in our community (e.g., *doctor, firefighter, paramedic*).

- Challenge students to write sentences with proper and common nouns. For example: *Officer Smith is a police officer in my town.*

Fluency

- Reread the poem in unison with students. Ask students to pay close attention to the sound of your voice. As you read the poem, change the volume of your voice from a whisper to a shout.

- Continue modeling the phrasing of the poem. Students will enjoy this activity, and you may want students to lead the class.

Comprehension

- Tell students that they will collect information about their class. Ask students to name their favorite drinks. Chart students' answers and tally their responses.

- Help students create a bar graph reflecting the favorite drinks of the class.

- Repeat the process with the question, "What does your mom want you to drink?" Compare the two graphs. Ask students why they think the graphs are similar or different. Have students write their responses.

Word Study Extension

Use page 55 to extend word concepts from the poem.

Soda Pop

Soda, soda, soda pop,

Drink it always, never stop.

Buy some soda when you shop.

Don't run out of soda pop!

Cherry, root beer, lemon-lime—

All day long it's soda time.

Get the nurse to call the cop,

I think my tummy's gonna pop!

—Tim Rasinski

Name: _____

Word Families

Directions: Use the letters from the Sound Bank to place in front of -op or -out to make new words. Write the words in the boxes.

-op	*-out*

Sound Bank

sh   m   p   ch   st   sl   h   cl

Write two sentences using words from the word families boxes.

1. _____

2. _____

•••

Challenge: Use the words you found to write an ad for a new kind of soda pop.

Name: _____

Word Building

I. Directions: *Write words from the poem in the correct groups. Then add new words to each group.*

Words with **-op**	Words with **-ime**	Words with **-ver**	Words About Soda

II. Directions: *Read each sentence. Write the missing word. Use the Word Bank for help.*

1. *I like _____ better than gold.*

2. *Two nickels make a _____.*

3. *I was so tired, I _____ right into bed.*

4. *Green _____ oozed from the ground.*

Word Bank

flopped   silver   dime   slime

The Wind Will Blow

See pages 10–11 for ideas to introduce the poem. Complete some or all of the following activities throughout the week. The activities on this page may be completed before, during, or after reading the poem. Select activities based on your students' needs.

Phonemic Awareness

- Tell students that you are going to say three words. They are to tell you which sound the words have in common.
- Say the words *will, bell,* and *pull.* Students should identify the /l/ sound as the sound the words have in common.
- Continue with the words below:

  swim, sum, mom—last sound is /m/

  whip, shop, sip—last sound is /p/

  run, ban, bin—last sound is /n/

Phonics

- Write the words *idea* and *pilot* on the board or on a sheet of chart paper. Explain to students that the letter *i* in each word makes the /ī/ sound. Ask students to use a green crayon to underline the /ī/ words in the poem (*ice, I*).
- Write the words *shin* and *bin* on the board or on a sheet of chart paper. Explain to students that the letter *i* in each word makes the /ĭ/ sound. Ask students to use a red crayon to underline the /ĭ/ words in the poem (*wind, will, fish, swim*).
- Encourage students to create more /ĭ/ words by adding, removing, and/or changing letters in the words they found in the poem. For example, the letter *d* can be removed from *wind* to create *win.*

Vocabulary

- Discuss with students the term *past tense* (a verb tense that expresses an action or a condition that occurred during the past). Tell students, "The girl runs to her friend." Ask students to identify the verb. Students should respond *runs.* Then ask students to change the verb to past tense. Students should respond *ran.*
- Explain that in the poem, the author says, "The fish will swim down very low." Ask students to say the past tense of the verb *swim.* Students should respond *swam.*
- Ask students to say the past tense of the following verbs: *speak, sleep,* and *give.*

Fluency

- Divide the class into two groups. Assign one stanza to each group.
- Ask the first group to practice reading as if they are being blown away. Ask the second group to practice reading as if they are underwater. Have the groups switch stanzas.

Comprehension

- Ask students to brainstorm words related to winter. Record students' responses.
- Distribute copies of page 58. Ask students to label the winter scene and write three sentences using winter words.

Word Study Extension

Use page 59 to extend word concepts from the poem.

The Wind Will Blow

The wind will blow
Over fields of snow,
And ice will form
Where waters flow.

And deep below
The ice and snow,
The fish will swim
Down very low.

And as they go
I want to know,
Do they stay warm
Down, down so low?

—Karen McGuigan Brothers

Name: _____

Winter Words

Directions: Use the Word Bank to label the winter picture with the correct words. Color the picture when you have labeled it.

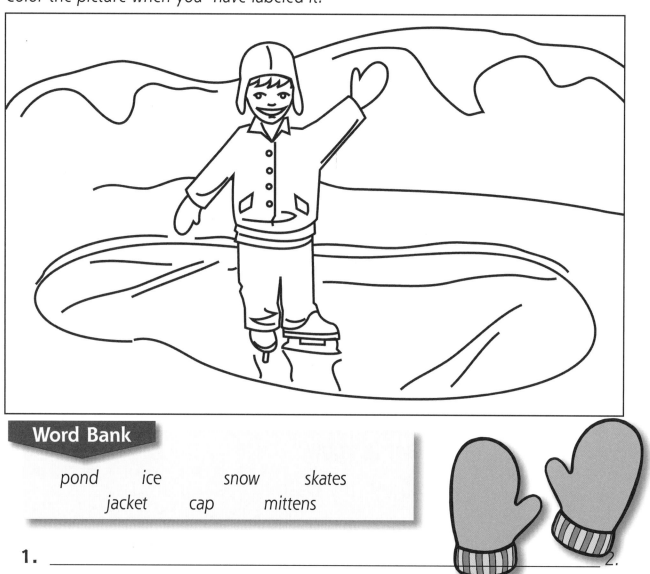

Word Bank

pond	ice	snow	skates
jacket	cap	mittens	

1. _____

2. ____

- -

Challenge: Write the letters A to Z on a sheet of paper. For each letter, think of a word about winter.

Name: _____

Word Building

I. Directions: Write words from the poem in the correct groups. Then add new words to each group.

Words with -*ow*	Words with -*ice*	Words with -*im*	Words About Fish

• •

II. Directions: Read each sentence. Write the missing word. Use the Word Bank for help.

1. Mom lets me _____ the bread at home.

2. The guests threw _____ at the bride and groom.

3. I _____ where Jake lives.

4. _____ drank milk with his lunch.

Word Bank

know   slice   rice   Tim

Happy Birthday to Me

See pages 10–11 for ideas to introduce the poem. Complete some or all of the following activities throughout the week. The activities on this page may be completed before, during, or after reading the poem. Select activities based on your students' needs.

Phonemic Awareness

- Tell students that you are going to say three words. They are to tell you which word doesn't belong or sounds different from the other words.

- Say the words *meet, see,* and *seal.* Students should respond that *meet* doesn't belong because it doesn't begin with /s/.

- Continue with the words listed below:

  sing, sit, win—win doesn't belong

  play, date, place—date doesn't belong

  fate, chair, chase—fate doesn't belong

Phonics

- Ask students to create a word family by adding letters to the beginning of the rime *-op.* Write students' responses on the board or on a sheet of chart paper (e.g., *pop, hop, stop, mop, drop, slop, top*).

- Ask students to select three of the words listed to write sentences. Have students share their sentences with a classmate.

Vocabulary

- Ask students to reread the poem and identify the nouns and verbs that are associated with birthdays.

- Tell students to fold a paper in half to record the nouns and verbs that they find in the poem (e.g., nouns—*candles, cards, presents, chairs;* verbs—*playing, sitting, take, singing*).

Fluency

- Divide students into three groups. Assign each group one stanza of the poem.

- Ask students to describe how they feel as it gets closer to their birthdays. Have them practice reading the stanzas that they have been assigned as if they are excited about their birthdays.

- Assign each group a different stanza and repeat.

Comprehension

- Discuss with students the definition of the word *invitation.* Ask students to describe how an invitation looks. Tell students that they will create birthday invitations.

- Distribute copies of page 62.

Word Study Extension

Use page 63 to extend word concepts from the poem.

Happy Birthday to Me

A birthday cake with candles,
Happy birthday to me!
Lots of cards and presents
And all of them for me.
Streamers, poppers, and balloons
Decorate the place.
There's lots of food to feast on—
There is no empty space.

Playing musical chairs
'Til someone hollers "Stop!"
And sitting on balloons
Until they pop, pop, pop.
There are bowls of yummy ice cream
And lots of birthday cake.
There are goody bags with candy
For all my guests to take.

I'm surrounded by my friends
As far as I can see.
And soon they all begin to sing
A birthday song to me.
Right when the singing's over,
They give a great big cheer.
And then the party's over
Until this time next year!

—Karen McGuigan Brothers

Name: _____

My Birthday

Directions: Use the Word Bank to complete the sentences to write a birthday invitation.

Dear _____,

    Please come to my _____ party. We will play
_____ like musical chairs. We will eat
_____ and _____. Chocolate is
my favorite. After you sing _____ birthday to me, I will
_____ the candles. Then I can open my
_____. We will have lots of _____.

                Sincerely,

                _____

Word Bank

presents	fun	games	birthday
happy	cake	blow	ice cream

Challenge: On a separate sheet of paper, write about a birthday present you would like to receive.

Name: _____

Word Building

I. Directions: *Write words from the poem in the correct groups. Then add new words to each group.*

Words with **-ake**	Words with **-ee**	Words with **-air**	Words About Birthdays

II. Directions: *Read each sentence. Write the missing word. Use the Word Bank for help.*

1. *Don't _____ me up until noon.*

2. *The maple is my favorite _____.*

3. *I like to sit in my rocking _____.*

4. *The _____ are pretty, but they melt too fast.*

Word Bank

tree   wake   snowflakes   chair

Smelly Feet

See pages 10–11 for ideas to introduce the poem. Complete some or all of the following activities throughout the week. The activities on this page may be completed before, during, or after reading the poem. Select activities based on your students' needs.

Phonemic Awareness

- Tell students that you are going to say a word, one sound at a time. Have students blend the sounds together to make a word.

- Segment the words from the poem. Say /t/, /ā/, /m/. Students should respond with *tame*.

- Practice with the words listed below:

  /th/, /ĭ/, /n/, /k/—*think*

  /s/, /t/, /ŏ/, /m/, /p/—*stomp*

  /s/, /m/, /ĕ/, /l/—*smell*

Phonics

- Ask students to create a word family by adding letters to the consonant blend *st-*. Tell students to add the letters *ar*. Students should respond *star*.

- Distribute copies of page 66.

- Tell students to add ending rimes to initial blends to make words.

Vocabulary

- Write the following sentence on the board: *Stinky Pete has smelly feet.* Ask students to identify the adjectives (descriptive words) in the sentence. Students should respond with *stinky* and *smelly*.

- Tell students to write a sentence about themselves, using two adjectives. Encourage students to use a sentence pattern (e.g., *Beautiful Beth has long hair*).

- After students complete their sentences, make a class chart listing the adjectives.

Fluency

- Tell students to use a yellow crayon to underline the lines in the poem that begin with *Cover, Put, Stand,* and *Dunk*.

- Ask a student to read each of those lines. Have the remainder of the class read all of the other lines.

- After reading the poem, reassign the four individual lines and reread again. Encourage students to use hand motions to act out their lines.

Comprehension

- In the poem, the author gives three suggestions to deal with stinky feet. Ask students to identify these (*cover them with a big white sheet*, *put them in a pen with some sheep that bleat*, *dunk them in a pool at a swimming meet*).

- Ask students whether these suggestions will help eliminate the foot odor.

- Tell students to write three suggestions of their own in complete sentences. Insert these sentences into the poem. Ask students if they like the poem with the new lines. Why or why not?

Word Study Extension

Use page 67 to extend word concepts from the poem.

Smelly Feet

Smelly, smelly, smelly feet,
Got a very bad case of smelly feet.

Cover them up with a big white sheet.
Still can smell my smelly feet.
Put them in with sheep that bleat.
Still can smell those smelly feet.
Stand right next to stinky Pete.
Still can smell my smelly feet.
Dunk them at a swimming meet.
Still can smell those smelly feet.

Smelly, smelly, smelly feet,
Got a really bad case of smelly feet.

—Tim Rasinski

Name: _____

Blends

Directions: *Choose endings for the initial blends to make new words. You may use the ending with as many blends as possible. Write the new words in each foot shape. Before you begin, predict which blend will make the most words.*

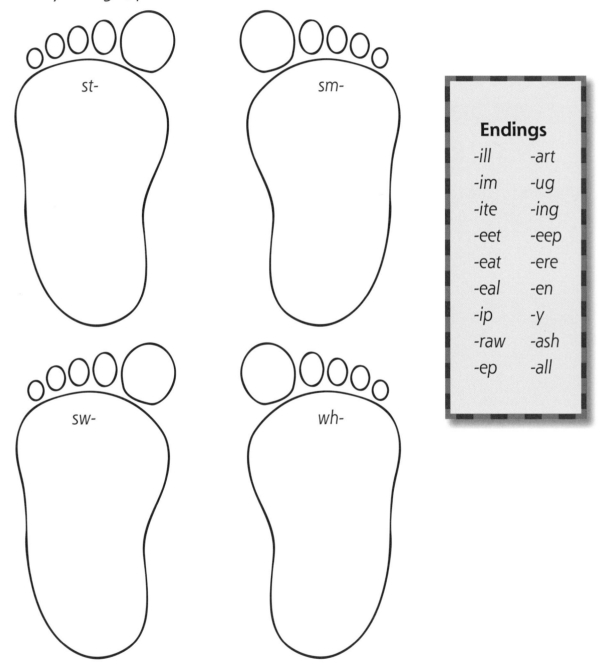

st-

sm-

sw-

wh-

Endings

-ill	-art
-im	-ug
-ite	-ing
-eet	-eep
-eat	-ere
-eal	-en
-ip	-y
-raw	-ash
-ep	-all

Challenge: *Use the words you created to write your own poem about stinky feet.*

Name: _____

Word Building

I. Directions: *Write words from the poem in the correct groups. Then add new words to each group.*

Words with *-eet*	Words with *-ell*	Words with *-ill*	Words About Smelly Feet

II. Directions: *Read each sentence. Write the missing word. Use the Word Bank for help.*

1. *I need two _____ of paper for my story.*

2. *Would you like to eat a _____ pickle?*

3. *Mom _____ me a story every night.*

4. *The navy has a _____ of ships.*

Word Bank

dill   fleet   sheets   tells

My Telephone

See pages 10–11 for ideas to introduce the poem. Complete some or all of the following activities throughout the week. The activities on this page may be completed before, during, or after reading the poem. Select activities based on your students' needs.

Phonemic Awareness

* Tell students that you are going to say a word, and they are to say the sounds they hear. Say the word *ring*. Students should respond /r/, /ĭ/, /n/, /g/. Ask students how many sounds are in the word *ring* (four).

* Practice with the following words:

  with—/w/, /ĭ/, /th/ (three)

  send—/s/, /ĕ/, /n/, /d/ (four)

  when—/wh/, /ĕ/, /n/ (three)

Phonics

* Distribute copies of page 70.

* Ask students to add *-ing* to the end of the words and then complete the sentences using the new words.

Vocabulary

* Ask students to brainstorm the parts of a telephone (e.g., *number buttons, earpiece, mouthpiece, antenna, cord, speaker, charger, caller ID, answering machine*).

* Ask students to complete the following sentences:

  I listen through the _____.

  I dial by pressing the _____.

  I speak into the _____.

* Use the words from the students' lists to make additional cloze sentences.

Fluency

* Tell students that they will practice phrasing by adding phrase boundaries to their poems.

* Guide students to add these phrase boundaries: My telephone has a ringer // I press numbers with my finger // Then I can talk / Or I can squawk / Or even be a singer //.

* Once students are finished adding phrase boundaries to their poems, have students practice reading independently, in pairs, or in groups.

Comprehension

* Reread the poem. Ask students to explain what the author is writing about (making a telephone call). As a class, write detailed directions for making a telephone call.

* Ask students to write detailed directions for tying shoelaces. After students finish writing their directions, encourage them to find a partner and exchange directions. Each student should follow his or her partner's directions to tie his or her shoelaces by doing only what is written.

Word Study Extension

Use page 71 to extend word concepts from the poem.

My Telephone

My telephone has a ringer.

I press numbers with my finger.

Then I can talk,

Or I can squawk,

Or even be a singer.

—Karen McGuigan Brothers

Name: _____

Telephone Endings

I. Directions: *Add -ing to the words in the box to create a new word.*

1. ring _____   **4.** squawk _____

2. sing _____   5. press _____

3. talk _____   6. tell _____

• •

II. Directions: *Use the words you created above to complete the sentences.*

7. Maria is _____ a song.

8. James is _____ the buttons on the telephone.

9. The telephone is _____ off the hook.

10. The bird is _____ in its cage.

11. Mom is _____ on the telephone.

12. Dad is _____ me to hang up the telephone.

• •

Challenge: *Make a list of 10 verbs. Exchange lists with a friend and add -ing to each verb.*

Name: _____

Word Building

I. Directions: *Write words from the poem in the correct groups. Then add new words to each group.*

Words with -inger	Words with -alk	Words with -ess	Words About Telephones

II. Directions: *Read each sentence. Write the missing word. Use the Word Bank for help.*

1. Grandma likes to _____ how tall I am.

2. Corn grows on a _____.

3. Beware of the _____ on the bee.

4. I broke my _____ when I fell.

Word Bank

stalk   finger   stinger   guess

Alphabet Rhyme

See pages 10–11 for ideas to introduce the poem. Complete some or all of the following activities throughout the week. The activities on this page may be completed before, during, or after reading the poem. Select activities based on your students' needs.

Phonemic Awareness

- Tell students that you will say some words. They are to identify the sound they hear at the beginning of each word. Ask students what sound they hear at the beginning of the word *sweet*. Students should respond /s/.
- Continue with the words listed below:

  trick—/t/ sound

  wish—/w/ sound

  black—/b/ sound

Phonics

- Tell students that when the letters *ee* are used in a word, they make the /ē/ vowel sound.
- Write the word *feet* on the board or on a sheet of chart paper. Point out the letters *ee*. Ask students to brainstorm other words with the letters *ee*. Record students' responses.
- Distribute copies of page 74.

Vocabulary

- Have students explore the prefix *dis-* by demonstrating the words *like* and *dislike*. Ask students how the word *like* changed with the addition of the prefix *dis-*.
- Ask students to use the word *dislike* in a sentence. (*The boy dislikes rain.*) Ask students what they think *dis-* means. (Dis- means "not" or "the opposite.")

- Ask students to add the prefix *dis-* to the following words and tell what the new word means:

  agree—*disagree* (not agree)

  able—*disable* (not able)

Fluency

- Tell students to circle the words and letters at the end of each line. Remind students that these sounds give clues for the words in the poem (*G* sounds like *tree*, *N* sounds like *in*, *T* sounds like *bee*, *Z* sounds like *me*).
- Ask students to read the poem several times. Each time, ask students to read the poem as if the line ends with a different punctuation mark (e.g., question mark, period, exclamation point, or comma).

Comprehension

- Write the following sentence on the board or on a sheet of chart paper: *If you plant a seed, then a tree will grow*. Explain to students that this is an example of a cause-and-effect statement.
- Ask students to brainstorm examples of cause and effect. (e.g., If you jump in a pool, *then* you will get wet.) Record students' examples and ask students to select or create an example to write and illustrate in their journals.

Word Study Extension

Use page 75 to extend word concepts from the poem.

Alphabet Rhyme

A-B-C-D-E-F-G,

Plant a seed and grow a tree.

H-I-J-K-L-M-N,

Open the door and let me in.

O-P-Q-R-S and T,

Get sweet honey from a bee.

U-V-W-X-Y and Z,

I like you, and you like me!

—Tim Rasinski

Name: _____

EE Puzzle

Directions: Use the words in the Word Bank to complete the sentences and write the words in the puzzle.

Across

3. Candy is _____.

5. I don't _____ well.

Down

1. A _____ can sting me.

2. Automobiles are made of _____.

3. I can plant a _____.

4. I climb up a _____.

5. It's time to _____ my cat.

Word Bank

steel	bee	feed	seed
feel	tree	sweet	

- -

Challenge: Make your own crossword puzzle using different ee words. Exchange your puzzle with a friend.

Name: _____

Word Building

I. Directions: *Write words from the poem in the correct groups. Then add new words to each group.*

Words with *-ike*	Words with *-eed*	Words with *-eet*	Words That Rhyme

II. Directions: *Read each sentence. Write the missing word. Use the Word Bank for help.*

1. The rain turned to _____.

2. I try to do a good _____ every day.

3. We had to _____ up the hill.

4. I rode my _____ to school.

Word Bank

bike   sleet   deed   hike

Number Rhyme

See pages 10–11 for ideas to introduce the poem. Complete some or all of the following activities throughout the week. The activities on this page may be completed before, during, or after reading the poem. Select activities based on your students' needs.

Phonemic Awareness

- Tell students that you are going to say three words. They are to tell you the sound the words have in common. Say the words *chick, chance,* and *choice.* Students should identify /ch/ as the initial sound in all three words.

- Continue with the words listed below:

  duckling, dance, doughnut—/d/ sound

  sheep, ship, shell—/sh/ sound

  thank, thumb, thick—/th/ sound

Phonics

- Have students chant the nursery rhyme "One, Two, Buckle My Shoe": *One, two, buckle my shoe; three, four, shut the door; five, six, pick up sticks; seven, eight, shut the gate; nine, ten, a big fat hen.* Say the poem several times and have students act out the words.

- Ask students to identify the numbers and words that rhyme (*two/shoe, four/door, six/sticks, eight/gate,* and *ten/hen*).

Vocabulary

- Ask students to brainstorm farm animals. Record students' responses.

- Select an animal listed and write a matching description. For example: This animal is spotted black and white and gives milk.) Tell students to think of other descriptions to match the animals listed.

- Distribute copies of page 78.

- Tell students that they will choose a word from the Word Bank to match the animal clue provided for the animal.

Fluency

- Have students practice high-frequency words (e.g., *about, seven, eight, better, only, laugh, together, start, light, carry*) by underlining them in their poems.

- Ask students to read the sentences containing the underlined words.

Comprehension

- Reread the poem. Draw students' attention to the last two lines of the poem: *Many baby animals, no time to sleep!* Ask students what the author meant by this statement. Are there hints in the poem?

- Ask students to write an explanation of what the author meant by the last line of the poem.

Word Study Extension

Use page 79 to extend word concepts from the poem.

Number Rhyme

1, 2, 3,

4, 5, 6,

7 little ducklings,

8 tiny chicks,

9 baby horses,

10 newborn sheep—

Many baby animals,

No time to sleep!

—Tim Rasinski

Name: _____

Farm Animals

Directions: *Read each sentence carefully. Choose a word from the Word Bank to match the animal to the sentence clue.*

1. This animal has wings and can swim in a pond. _____

2. This animal has a coat of wool. _____

3. This animal has a curly tail. _____

4. This animal lays eggs for my breakfast. _____

5. This animal can give me a ride on its back. _____

6. This animal gives milk for me to drink. _____

7. This animal barks at strangers. _____

8. This animal has long ears and hops. _____

Word Bank

pig	horse
hen	sheep
dog	rabbit
duck	cow

Name: _____

Word Building

I. Directions: *Write words from the poem in the correct groups. Then add new words to each group.*

Words with **-eep**	Words with **-ings**	Words with **-ick**	Words About Animals

II. Directions: *Read each sentence. Write the missing word. Use the Word Bank for help.*

1. *I count _____ when I can't sleep.*

2. *I can hear _____ cluck.*

3. *An airplane has two _____ .*

4. *The hill was too _____ to climb.*

Word Bank

chickens   steep   wings   sheep

Opposites

See pages 10–11 for ideas to introduce the poem. Complete some or all of the following activities throughout the week. The activities on this page may be completed before, during, or after reading the poem. Select activities based on your students' needs.

Phonemic Awareness

- Tell students that you are going to say three words. They are to tell you the word that doesn't belong or sounds different from the other words.

- Say the words *top*, *shop*, and *pot*. Students should identify that *pot* doesn't belong because it doesn't end with the /p/ sound.

- Continue with the words listed below:

  of, shout, out—of doesn't end with /t/

  last, class, past—class doesn't end with /t

  spin, win, pit—pit doesn't end with /n/

Phonics

- Tell students that they will investigate the "final *e* rule" by demonstrating the change of the vowel sound from short to long.

- Tell students that the word *fin* changes to *fine* when the letter *e* is added. Practice with the following words:

  Tim—add *e* (time)

  pin—add *e* (pine)

  bit—add *e* (bite)

Vocabulary

- Explain to students that another name for an opposite word is an *antonym*. Give examples such as *big/small* and *hot/cold*.

- Distribute copies of page 82.

- Tell students that they will read the words in each box and write the antonym for that word.

Fluency

- Read the poem together as a class. Ask students to identify the antonyms in the poem. Write them on a chart for an ongoing collection of opposites.

- Divide the class into five groups. Assign a line or lines containing opposite words from the poem to each group. Have students read their line(s) and create a hand or body motion to illustrate the opposite words.

- After all of the groups have practiced, have students perform the poem, each group reciting and acting out their lines. Have all students read the last line together.

Comprehension

- On the board or on a sheet of chart paper, write: *What is the opposite of tall?* Record students' responses (*short* is a possible answer).

- Ask students to say a word that means the same as *tall* (*high* is a possible answer). Remind students that another name for an opposite word is an *antonym* and another name for a word that means the same is a *synonym*. Ask students to look for antonyms in the poem. Tell students that they will rewrite the poem by replacing the antonyms with synonyms.

Word Study Extension

Use page 83 to extend word concepts from the poem.

Opposites

Top and bottom,

In and out,

Time for quiet,

Time to shout!

Fast and slow,

Black and white,

Tall and short,

Day and night.

Full and empty,

First and last,

Opposites—

Oh, what a blast!

—Tim Rasinski

Name: _____

Blast Off

Directions: Read each word and choose its opposite from the words in the Word Bank. Write the opposite word in the rocket ship.

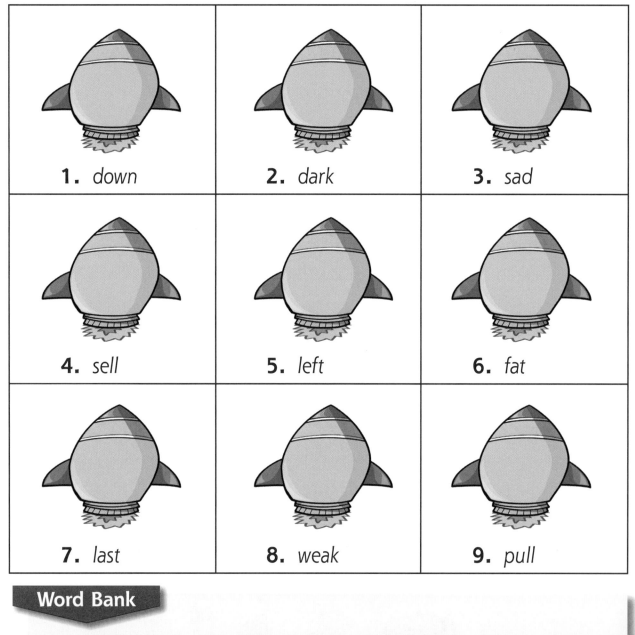

1. down

2. dark

3. sad

4. sell

5. left

6. fat

7. last

8. weak

9. pull

Word Bank

happy   up   first   thin   light   right   strong   push   buy

Challenge: Write a sentence for each pair of opposites.

Name: _____

Word Building

I. Directions: Write words from the poem in the correct groups. Then add new words to each group.

Words with **-ast**	Words with **-out**	Words with **-ull**	Words that are Opposites

II. Directions: Read each sentence. Write the missing word. Use the Word Bank for help.

1. My dad took me _____ fishing last week.

2. My stomach is _____ from eating too much!

3. The rocket _____ off this morning.

4. The tow truck _____ the car.

Word Bank

full   blasted   trout   pulled

Growing Up

See pages 10–11 for ideas to introduce the poem. Complete some or all of the following activities throughout the week. The activities on this page may be completed before, during, or after reading the poem. Select activities based on your students' needs.

Phonemic Awareness

- Tell students that you will say a word and they are to identify the vowel sound in the word. Say the word *fox*. Students should respond with the /ŏ/ sound.

- Distribute copies of page 86.

- Have students look at each picture, say the word aloud, and identify the vowel sound in each word.

Phonics

- Tell students that they will identify and circle the short vowel words in the poem. Have students use a red crayon for the *short u* word (puppy), a blue crayon for the *short o* words (dog, hog), a green crayon for the *short i* words (kitty, piggy), and a yellow crayon for the *short a* words (cat, brat).

- Make class charts to add words to each of these categories (short vowels *u, o, i, a*). Ask students to predict which category will have the most words after adding to the charts for one week.

Vocabulary

- Write the words *kitten*, *pup*, and *piglet* on the board or on a sheet of chart paper. Ask students what the words have in common. (They are names for baby animals.)

- Explain to students that the author says a puppy becomes a dog in the poem. Use that format for students to identify the following animals:

  A calf becomes a cow.

  A foal becomes a horse.

  A duckling becomes a duck.

  A fry becomes a fish.

  A kid becomes a goat.

Fluency

- Ask students to read with you as you repeatedly read the poem, using different intonations and volume.

- Encourage students to reread the poem in pairs. Have one student be the reader and the other the listener. After three readings, have students switch.

Comprehension

- Ask students to tell you who is speaking in the poem (the author). How does the author feel about her brother? Does she like him? How do you know?

- Explain to students the author implies she does not like her brother. Ask students to write about something they like without using the words *I* and *like*.

Word Study Extension

Use page 87 to extend word concepts from the poem.

Growing Up

A puppy becomes a dog.

A kitty becomes a cat.

A piggy becomes a hog.

Baby brother becomes a brat.

—Karen McGuigan Brothers

Name: _____

Listen Up

Directions: *Look at the pictures. Say each one aloud. Write the vowel you hear in the box in the corner.*

1. 	2. 	3.	4. 
		10	

5. 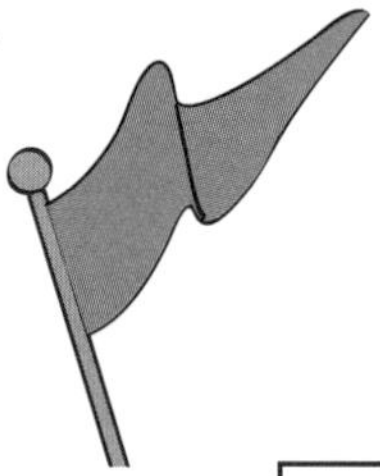	6. 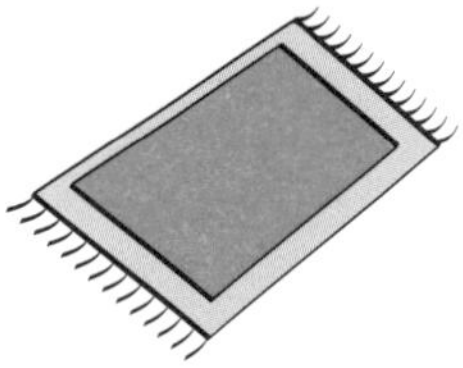	7. 	8. 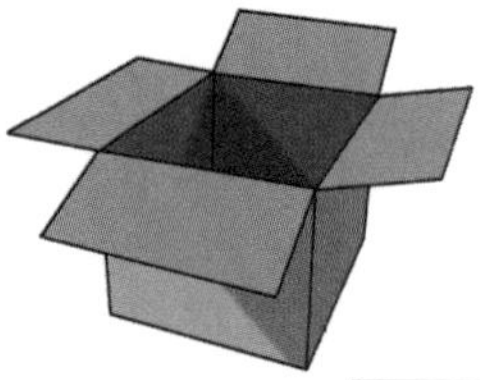

9. 	10. 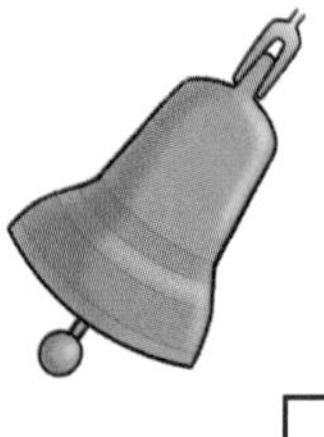	11. 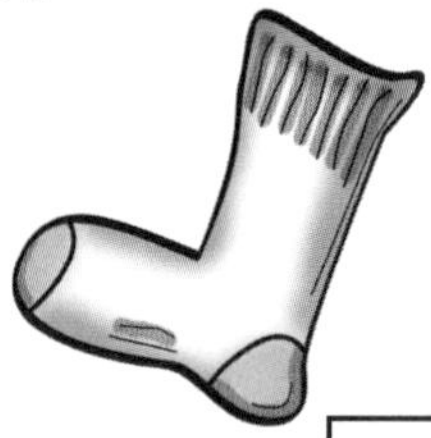	12. 

Vowel Bank

a   e   i   o   u

Challenge: *Write a silly sentence that has words with all the short vowel sounds.*

Name: _____

Word Building

I. Directions: *Write words from the poem in the correct groups. Then add new words to each group.*

Words with *-at*	Words with *-og*	Words with *-up*	Words About Growing Up

II. Directions: *Read each sentence. Write the missing word. Use the Word Bank for help.*

1. We got _____ down in heavy traffic.

2. The cat ate my new _____ .

3. The baby lost his _____.

4. Six _____ raced to the finish line.

Word Bank

guppy   runners   rattle   bogged

My Blanket

See pages 10–11 for ideas to introduce the poem. Complete some or all of the following activities throughout the week. The activities on this page may be completed before, during, or after reading the poem. Select activities based on your students' needs.

Phonemic Awareness

- Tell students that you will say a word very slowly, one sound at a time. Have students blend the sounds together to make a word.

- Segment the words from the poem by saying the sounds one sound at a time. Say /w/, /i/, /th/. Students should respond with *with*.

- Practice with the words listed below:

  /f/, /ō/, /l/, /d/—*fold*

  /v/, /ĕ/, /r/, /ē/—*very*

  /b/, /or/, /n/—*born*

  /d/, /ā/—*day*

Phonics

- Write the blend *bl-* on the board or on a sheet of chart paper. Ask students to brainstorm words that begin with this blend. Record students' responses.

- Put students in groups of four. Have them list words that begin with the *bl-* blend. After three to five minutes, ask the groups to read their words to the class. Record all of the words on the board or on a sheet of chart paper. As words are repeated, circle the words that appear more than once on the list.

Vocabulary

- Ask students to list words that relate to getting ready to go to bed (e.g., *pajamas, pillow, bedroom, slippers*). Record students' responses. Encourage students to group the words into three categories.

- Distribute copies of page 90.

- Ask students to organize the nighttime words in the Word Bank into different categories.

Fluency

- Have students reread the poem aloud. Ask students to look for five interesting or unknown words in the poem and write them on a sheet of paper or in a journal.

- Tell students that they will work in small groups to discuss the words listed and their possible definitions. Have the groups practice reading the poem in stanzas.

Comprehension

- Ask students different types of questions, both explicit and implicit, about the poem: What color is the blanket? What is on the edges of the blanket? Why do you think that the blanket is worn? Where is the blanket now? What are 'baby things'? Is the author still a baby? How old do you think the author is?

- For the inferential questions, ask students what information in the poem helped them with their answers.

Word Study Extension

Use page 91 to extend word concepts from the poem.

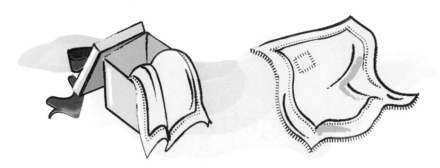

My Blanket

There is a yellow blanket
I got when I was born,
With satin all around it—
Though now it's very worn.

It's folded in the closet
With other baby things,
Like baby shirts and nightgowns
And even teething rings.

Sometimes when I get tired
And my day is at an end,
I take my baby blanket out
And sleep with it again.

—Karen McGuigan Brothers

Name: _____

Nighttime

Directions: *Organize your thoughts. Categorize the nighttime words from the Word Bank. Some words may be used more than once.*

Things I need

Things I do

Places I sleep

Word Bank

sleep	slippers	bathe	teddy bear	bed
bedroom	blanket	pillow	parents' room	bath
pajamas	toothbrush	couch	good-night kiss	

Challenge: Group the words from the Word Bank in a different way.

Name: _____

Word Building

I. Directions: *Write words from the poem in the correct groups. Then add new words to each group.*

Words with *-orn*	Words with *-end*	Words with *-ing*	Words About Old Things

II. Directions: *Read each sentence. Write the missing word. Use the Word Bank for help.*

1. My _____ and I like to play games together.

2. I was _____ in a hospital.

3. When my hand fell asleep, it began to _____.

4. My best friend lives just around the _____.

Word Bank

born   friends   corner   tingle

Yum Yum

See pages 10–11 for ideas to introduce the poem. Complete some or all of the following activities throughout the week. The activities on this page may be completed before, during, or after reading the poem. Select activities based on your students' needs.

Phonemic Awareness

- Tell students that you are going to say a word, and they are to break the word into its sounds by snapping, clapping, and tapping the sounds they hear.
- Say the word *red*. Students should respond /r/ (snap) /ĕ/ (clap) /d/.
- Practice with the following words:

  sun—/s/ clap /ŭ/ tap /n/ snap

  jet—/j/ clap /ĕ/ tap /t/ snap

  ran—/r/ clap /ă/ tap /n/ snap

  mop—/m/ clap /ŏ/ tap /p/ snap

Phonics

- Ask students to look for words in the poem that end in the letter *y* (*tasty, juicy, many,* and *tummy*). Explain to students that a word ending with the letter *y* makes the /ē/ sound.
- Tell students to brainstorm other words that end with the /ē/ sound. Write students' responses on the board or on a sheet of chart paper. Do those words end with a *y*? (Hint: not all do.)

Vocabulary

- Tell students that the poem has some descriptive words (e.g., *juicy, tasty, ripe*). Explain that another name for a descriptive word is an *adjective*.
- Distribute copies of page 94.
- Tell students that they will complete the activity to practice using adjectives in sentences.

Fluency

- Tell students that they are going to echo-read the poem (read the same line after the teacher reads it), mimicking the intonation and phrasing. Read the poem to students in a normal voice. Then echo-read the poem by reading a line and having students read it back.
- After students practice reading the poem three times, have students echo-read in pairs.

Comprehension

- Ask students to name different types of fruit. Write students' answers on the board or on a sheet of chart paper.
- Tell students that they will work in pairs to name the fruits they like and dislike. Ask students to write new versions of the poem, either agreeing or disagreeing with the author's perspective on liking fruit. Share the new versions with the class.

Word Study Extension

Use page 95 to extend word concepts from the poem.

Yum Yum

Red, ripe apples,

Juicy grapes,

Tasty fruit

In many shapes.

Juicy peaches,

Purple plums,

Make my tummy

Go yum yum!

—Tim Rasinski

Name: _____

Describing Words

Directions: *The first two words in each phrase below are describing words (adjectives). Add a noun from the Word Bank to the end of the describing words below.*

1. a tall, green _____

2. a scary, brown _____

3. a soft, furry _____

4. a round, bouncy _____

5. a sweet, chewy _____

6. a fast, shiny _____

Word Bank

bear   rabbit   candy   car   tree   ball

Complete the sentences with the adjectives from the phrases above.

7. Jason ate a _____ candy.

8. Scott has a _____ rabbit for a pet.

9. I like to play with the _____ ball.

10. Dad drives a _____ car.

11. A _____ bear climbed a _____ tree.

Name: _____

Word Building

I. Directions: Write words from the poem in the correct groups. Then add new words to each group.

Words with *-ape*	Words with *-um*	Words with *-each*	Words About Fruit

II. Directions: Read each sentence. Write the missing word. Use the Word Bank for help.

1. I love to hear the waves crash on the _____.

2. The superhero wore a red _____.

3. We had to _____ water out of our basement.

4. _____ person in our family is important.

Word Bank

pump   cape
Each   beach

Animal Stew

See pages 10–11 for ideas to introduce the poem. Complete some or all of the following activities throughout the week. The activities on this page may be completed before, during, or after reading the poem. Select activities based on your students' needs.

Phonemic Awareness

- Tell students that you will say some words. They are to identify the sound they hear at the ending of each word. Ask students what sound they hear at the end of the word *animal*. Students should respond /l/.

- Continue with the words listed below:

  horse—/s/   *barn*—/n/

  chick—/k/   *coop*—/p/

Phonics

- Write the rime *-ew* on the board or on a sheet of chart paper. Tell students that the title of the poem has the word *stew*, which has the rime *-ew*.

- Ask students to make new words by adding letters to the rime. Write students' responses on the board or on a sheet of chart paper (e.g., *blew, flew, new, dew*).

Vocabulary

- Ask students to reread the third line in the poem (*Horses make radish*). Ask what the author means by this.

- Explain that the author is making a word play with *horseradish*. *Horseradish* is a compound word made from two words in the poem: *horse* and *radish*. Have students create more compound words using the following words:

  stop + light = stoplight

  dog + house = doghouse

  house + fly = housefly

Fluency

- Distribute copies of page 98.

- Ask students to cut out the book pattern on the dashed lines and fold to place the pages in order. Tell students that they will work in pairs to illustrate and then practice reading the poem.

Comprehension

- Distribute a blank sheet of paper to each student. Ask students to draw a square about the size of their fists in the middle of the paper.

- Tell students to listen carefully as you give directions for the picture. State the following directions:

  Draw a horse inside the square.

  Draw a tree to the right of the square.

  Draw a triangle on top of the square.

  Draw a chicken inside the triangle.

  Draw three flowers to the left of the square.

- Read the poem aloud. Have students compare the drawings to the one that you make on the board or sheet of chart paper after giving the directions.

Word Study Extension

Use page 99 to extend word concepts from the poem.

Animal Stew

Horses in the barn

Chickens in the coop;

Horses make radish.

Chickens make soup.

—Karen McGuigan Brothers

Name: _____

Poem Book

Directions: Cut out the book pattern on the dashed lines. Fold the book to place pages in order. Illustrate each page to match the sentence. Read your poem book to three different classmates.

Horses in the barn

Chickens make soup.
—Tim Rasinski

Animal Stew

Chickens in the coop

Horses make radish.

Name: _____

Word Building

I. Directions: Write words from the poem in the correct groups. Then add new words to each group.

Words with **-oop**	Words with **-ish**	Words with **-ake**	Words About Farm Animals

• •

II. Directions: Read each sentence. Write the missing word. Use the Word Bank for help.

1. The dinner was served on new _____.

2. The chickens lived in a _____.

3. The _____ were high at the ball game.

4. Please put _____ in the salads.

Word Bank

coop   radishes
dishes   stakes

Camping

See pages 10–11 for ideas to introduce the poem. Complete some or all of the following activities throughout the week. The activities on this page may be completed before, during, or after reading the poem. Select activities based on your students' needs.

Phonemic Awareness

- Tell students that you will say three words. They are to identify the sound that the words have in common. Say the words *tent*, *net*, and *night*. Students should respond /t/.

- Continue with the words listed below:

  listen, last, long—beginning /l/ sound

  bird, basket, bake—beginning /b/ sound

  vent, vet, vehicle—beginning /v/ sound

  tune, stun, spin—ending /n/ sound

Phonics

- Tell students to circle the words in the poem that end with *-ing* (*sleeping, listening, twinkling, hearing, crackling, camping*).

- Ask students to brainstorm other verbs with the *-ing* suffix (e.g., *running*, *jumping*, *playing*). Record students' responses. After the list has been created, encourage students to act out the verbs.

Vocabulary

- Tell students that the name of the poem is "Camping." Discuss with students what the word *camping* means to them.

- Ask students to draw pictures to match the word *camping*. Be sure that the pictures include the settings (where) and what the students would need for sleeping, eating, and activities. After the pictures are complete, have students label the items.

Fluency

- Write the following phrase on the board or on a sheet of chart paper: *Here we go*. Tell students that the phrase contains a sight word that is in the poem (*here*).

- Write the following phrases below to continue practicing recognizing sight words that are in the poem:

  through the woods

  under the sea

  many things to do

  by myself

  With practice, students will quickly recognize the words in their reading.

Comprehension

- Ask students if they have ever gone camping. Discuss the activities you can do when camping (e.g., hiking, making s'mores, singing by the campfire).

- Distribute copies of page 102.

- Tell students they will use the poem to answer the questions.

Word Study Extension

Use page 103 to extend word concepts from the poem.

Camping

Sleeping in my sleeping bag
Here inside the tent,
Softly now the night breeze blows,
Through a netted vent.
Listening to the crickets sing
A joyful all-night tune,
Twinkling stars fill up the sky
Lit brightly by the moon.
Hearing the crackling of the fire
And the night bird's peaceful song,
Camping is my favorite thing
To do all summer long.

—Karen McGuigan Brothers

Name: _____

Looking Back and More

Directions: Use the poem "Camping" to answer the questions in complete sentences.

1. Where was the sleeping bag? _____

   _____

2. What was singing? _____

   _____

3. Was it day or night? _____

   _____

4. What was in the sky? _____

   _____

5. What sound did the campfire make? _____

   _____

6. What season was it? _____

   _____

7. Did the author like camping? Why? _____

   _____

8. Would you like to go camping? Why or why not? _____

   _____

Name: _____

Word Building

I. Directions: *Write words from the poem in the correct groups. Then add new words to each group.*

Words with *-ong*	Words with *-oon*	Words with *-une*	Words About Camping

II. Directions: *Read each sentence. Write the missing word. Use the Word Bank for help.*

1. *I love to hear singers* _____ .

2. My favorite movie is_____ .

3. In _____, summer vacation begins.

4. The _____ made it as bright as day.

Word Bank

King Kong   moonlight   croon   June

Ten

See pages 10–11 for ideas to introduce the poem. Complete some or all of the following activities throughout the week. The activities on this page may be completed before, during, or after reading the poem. Select activities based on your students' needs.

Phonemic Awareness

- Tell students that you are going to say a word, and then ask them to add a new beginning sound to make a new word. Say *air*. Have students add /p/ to *air* (*pair*).
- Distribute copies of page 106.
- Tell students to make new words by adding new sounds to the beginning of the words.

Phonics

- Write the following on the board or on a sheet of chart paper: *t__n*. Ask students what letters can be written in the blank to make new words (e.g, *ten, ton, tin, tan*).
- Continue the process with the following:

  b__g: bag, beg, big, bug

  p__t: pat, pet, pit, pot, put

  f__t: fat, fit

Vocabulary

- Write the word *scout* on the board or on a sheet of chart paper. Ask students to give two definitions for the word *scout*. (e.g., 1. Someone sent out by a group to discover information; 2. To search or explore.)
- Have students write the following words on index cards: *pen, sink, light*. Read the following sentence frames and have students hold up the correct word card.

  Anne wrote with a _____.

  I wash my hands in the _____.

  I turn on the _____.

Fluency

- Read the poem with incorrect phrasing: Ten chickens make / a flock they / live inside / a coop one / boy makes a / scout ten boys/ make a troop//. Ask students if the poem sounds correct (no).
- Tell students that all the words are correct and in the correct order. Work through the poem orally and have students help you correct each phrase.

Comprehension

- Tell students that the author uses two *collective nouns*. Describe what a collective noun is (a noun that is singular in form but refers to a group of people or things). Ask students what the words *flock* and *troop* have in common.
- Challenge students to think of other collective nouns. Tell students to write the collective nouns on index cards and draw a picture to match the noun.

Word Study Extension

Use page 107 to extend word concepts from the poem.

Ten

Ten chickens make a flock.

They live inside a coop.

One boy makes a boy scout.

Ten boys make a troop.

—Tim Rasinski

Name: _____

Make New Words

I. Directions: *Add the letter to the word to make a new word.*

1. f + lock = _____ **4.** s + pot = _____

2. p + roof = _____ **5.** c + rock = _____

3. s + can = _____ **6.** s + lid = _____

II. Directions: *Change one letter in the word to make a new word for the next car.*

7.

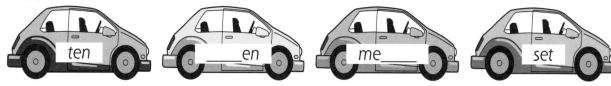

ten   _____en   me_____   set

8.

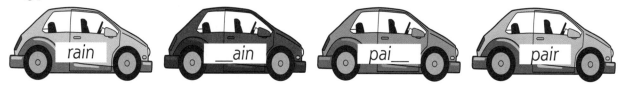

rain   ___ain   pai___   pair

9.

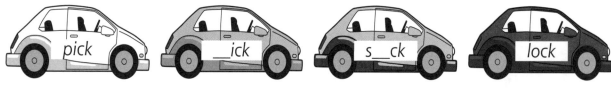

pick   ___ick   s___ck   lock

10.

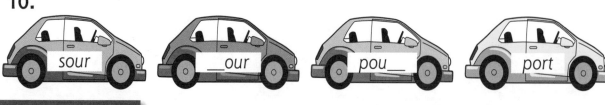

sour   ___our   pou___   port

Word Bank

met   pain   sick   men   pail   pout   sock   pour

Name: _____

Word Building

I. Directions: *Write words from the poem in the correct groups. Then add new words to each group.*

Words with *-ock*	Words with *-out*	Words with *-en*	Words About Numbers

II. Directions: *Read each sentence. Write the missing word. Use the Word Bank for help.*

1. The Cub _____ meet at my house.

2. Be sure to _____ your doors.

3. Do you know _____ the game begins?

4. Mom was _____ by my report card.

Word Bank

lock　　shocked　　when　　Scouts

Hula-Hoop

See pages 10–11 for ideas to introduce the poem. Complete some or all of the following activities throughout the week. The activities on this page may be completed before, during, or after reading the poem. Select activities based on your students' needs.

Phonemic Awareness

- Tell students that you will say a word and then ask them to remove the beginning sound to make a new word. Ask students to say *hand* without /h/. Students should respond *and*.

- Practice with the words listed below:

  drink without /d/—*rink*

  skid without /s/—*kid*

  play without /p/—*lay*

Phonics

- Have students compare the two sounds that the letters *oo* make. Write the words *look* and *hoop* on the board or on a sheet of chart paper. Point out that the words share the same middle letters, but the letters make a different sound.

- Ask students to brainstorm other words that have the double *o* letters (*e.g., cook, book, coop, troop, loom, broom*). Record students' responses.

Vocabulary

- Write the sentence *I really like to hula-hoop!* on the board or on a sheet of chart paper. Ask students to think of another word to use instead of *like* in the sentence (*e.g., enjoy, love*).

- Tell students that words with the same meanings are called *synonyms*. Work as a class to make a list of synonyms for the following words: *rock, difficult, bucket, large, noon, clean, noise,* and *sick*.

Fluency

- Tell students that they are going to echo-read the poem (read the same line after the teacher reads it), mimicking the intonation and phrasing. Read the poem to students in a normal voice. Then echo-read the poem by reading a line and having students read it back.

- Distribute copies of page 110.

- Have students use the phrase marks to read the poem with the proper phrasing.

Comprehension

- Ask students what the author likes to do in the poem (hula-hoop). If they could talk to the author, what questions would they ask him about the hula-hoop? Write the students' questions on the board or on a sheet of chart paper. (Possible questions students may ask: How did you learn to hula-hoop? Why do you like to hula-hoop?)

- Have students work in pairs to brainstorm possible answers for the questions created.

Word Study Extension

Use page 111 to extend word concepts from the poem.

Hula-Hoop

Hula, hula, hula-hoop,

Cha-cha-cha and loop-de-loop,

By myself and in a group,

I really like to hula-hoop!

—Tim Rasinski

Name: _____

Say It Well

Directions: *Use the phrase marks to help you read the poem with the proper phrasing. The **I** indicates a short pause. The **II** indicates a full stop of your voice. Practice reading the poem several times.*

Hula-Hoop

Hula, **I** hula, **I** hula-hoop, **II**

Cha-cha-cha **I** and loop-de-loop, **II**

By myself **I** and in a group, **II**

I really like **I** to hula-hoop! **II**

—Tim Rasinski

Name: _____

Word Building

I. Directions: *Write words from the poem in the correct groups. Then add new words to each group.*

Words with **-ike**	Words with **-oop**	Words with **-oup**	Words About Sports

II. Directions: *Read each sentence. Write the missing word. Use the Word Bank for help.*

1. *She had* _____ *for lunch.*

2. *Mom said, "* _____ *" when she dropped the glass.*

3. *I* _____ *panda bears.*

4. *A chicken lives in a* _____ *.*

Word Bank

Whoops   like   soup   coop

Grape Pop

See pages 10–11 for ideas to introduce the poem. Complete some or all of the following activities throughout the week. The activities on this page may be completed before, during, or after reading the poem. Select activities based on your students' needs.

Phonemic Awareness

- Tell students that you are going to say a word and then ask them to substitute sounds within the word to make a new word. Say *top*. Have students change the /t/ in *top* to /p/. Students should respond *pop*.

- Practice with the words listed below:

  Change the /ŏ/ in *drop* to /ĭ/—*drip*.

  Change the /p/ in *top* to /t/—*tot*.

  Change the /n/ in *man* to /p—map*.

Phonics

- Tell students they will investigate the final *e* rule by demonstrating the change of the vowel sound from short to long. Tell students the word *fin* changes to *fine* when the letter *e* is added.

- Distribute copies of page 114.

- Have students add the letter *e* to make new words.

Vocabulary

- Have students reread the poem. Grape pop is one of the author's favorite things. Ask students to brainstorm their favorite things to eat or drink. Write students' responses on the board or on a sheet of chart paper.

- Encourage students to use the following cloze sentence for students to explain their favorite foods:

  One of my favorite foods is _____ because _____.

Fluency

- Tell students that they are going to echo-read the poem (read the same line after the teacher reads it), mimicking the intonation and phrasing. Read the poem to students in a normal voice. Then echo-read the poem by reading a line and having students read it back.

- After students practice reading the poem three times, have students echo-read in pairs.

Comprehension

- Ask students if grape pop is a good drink. Should the author drink grape pop? Why or why not?

- Ask students to write a paragraph for or against drinking grape pop.

Word Study Extension

Use page 115 to extend word concepts from the poem.

Grape Pop

Grape pop, grape pop,

I love to drink my grape pop.

Drink a whole bottle,

Or just sip a drop.

Any way you drink it

It's a mighty great pop—

Grape pop!

—Tim Rasinski

Name: _____

Final *e*

I. Directions: *Add a final e to make a new word.*

1. kit + e _____

2. can + e _____

3. hid + e _____

4. tap + e _____

5. plan + e _____

• •

II. Directions: *Use the new words to complete the sentences.*

6. *I have a plan to build a _____.*

7. *We played _____ and seek. My friend hid behind the tree.*

8. *Grandfather can walk with a _____.*

9. *I used _____ to wrap my sister's birthday present.*

10. *I bought a kit to make a _____.*

Name: _____

Word Building

I. Directions: *Write words from the poem in the correct groups. Then add new words to each group.*

Words with -op	Words with -ole	Words with -ink	Words About My Favorite Drink

II. Directions: *Read each sentence. Write the missing word. Use the Word Bank for help.*

1. Give him a bottle of _____.

2. The skunk made the neighborhood _____.

3. Dad dug a _____ in the backyard.

4. Someone _____ my new bike.

Word Bank

stink   stole   pop   hole

Sick Pet

See pages 10–11 for ideas to introduce the poem. Complete some or all of the following activities throughout the week. The activities on this page may be completed before, during, or after reading the poem. Select activities based on your students' needs.

Phonemic Awareness

- Tell students that you are going to say a word and then ask them to add a sound to the word to make a new word. Say *ill*. Have students add /p/ to the beginning of *ill*. Students should respond with *pill*.

- Practice with the words listed below:

  Add /t/ to *wig—twig*

  Add /s/ to *top—stop*

  Add /b/ to *link—blink*

  Add /g/ to *rip—grip*

Phonics

- Ask students to create a word family by adding letters to the beginning of the rime *-et*. Tell students to add the /b/ sound to *-et* (*bet*).

- Have students brainstorm other words that have the rime *-et*. Record students' responses. (Possible answers: *bet, vet, net, set, met,* and *wet.*)

Vocabulary

- Have students fold a sheet of paper to create two boxes. Have students write *doctor's office* in one box and *veterinarian's office* in the other box.

- Tell students to work in small groups to list objects they would find in each place. Have students share aloud the items from their lists (e.g., doctor—*receptionist, table, stethoscope, doctor, medicine, nurse;* veterinarian—*receptionist, dogs, cats, medicine, doctor, scale*).

Fluency

- Ask students if they have ever seen a "Lost Pet" sign before. What did it look like? What information did it have?

- Distribute copies of page 118.

- Tell students they will create a poster to help find a lost pet. Remind students to include a description and a picture.

- Have students work in pairs and have them practice reading their "Lost Pet" signs.

Comprehension

- Ask students to respond to questions verbally or in writing about the poem. What is a vet? (*animal doctor*) Who went to see the vet? (*a sick pet*) What kind of a pet went to see the vet? (*The author doesn't say.*) What did the vet give to the pet? (*a shot and a pill*) What is a shot? (*medicine given by injection*) Did the pet get better? (*Yes, the pet is no longer ill.*) Does the author love his pet? (*Yes, he took it to the vet when it was sick.*)

Word Study Extension

Use page 119 to extend word concepts from the poem.

Sick Pet

Sick pet, sick pet,

Had to go and see the vet.

Got a shot and then a pill.

Now, our pet's no longer ill.

—Tim Rasinski

Name: _____

Lost Pet

Directions: Create a poster to help find your lost pet. Remember to include a description and a picture of your pet.

Lost _____

Please help me find _____!

_____

_____

_____

_____

_____

_____

If found, please call _____.

Challenge: On a separate sheet of paper, write a story describing the adventures your pet had while it was lost.

Name: _____

Word Building

I. Directions: Write words from the poem in the correct groups. Then add new words to each group.

Words with **-ill**	Words with **-et**	Words with **-ot**	Words About Being Sick

II. Directions: Read each sentence. Write the missing word. Use the Word Bank for help.

1. I _____ six answers wrong on today's test.

2. The _____ on the stove is filled with soup.

3. Billy is sick and has the _____.

4. Our town was the _____ for every story we read in school.

Word Bank

kettle   chills   got   setting

Toucan

See pages 10–11 for ideas to introduce the poem. Complete some or all of the following activities throughout the week. The activities on this page may be completed before, during, or after reading the poem. Select activities based on your students' needs.

Phonemic Awareness

- Tell students that they will practice segmenting words into sounds by using the names of their families, friends, and pets.

- Have students work in small groups to segment a name (e.g., /j/, /ā/, /n/). The other students in the group will guess the person's or pet's name (*Jane*).

Phonics

- Have students reread the poem. Write the question, *Who can catch a toucan?* on the board or on a sheet of chart paper.

- Have students answer the question with words that rhyme with *can* (e.g., *Dan can catch a toucan; Stan can catch a toucan; The man can catch a toucan.*).

Vocabulary

- Play "What is it?" with students by giving clues about other things with wings.

- Say clues one at a time to reveal information about each thing. For example, with the word *toucan*, you can say it has wings, lives in a tree, and has a colorful beak. Have students guess the selected vocabulary word.

- Continue with the clues and vocabulary words below:

  It has wings. It carries people. (*airplane*)

  It has wings. It begins as a caterpillar. (*butterfly*)

  It has wings. It has sharp claws. Its babies are called eaglets. (*eagle*)

Fluency

- Tell students they will work in groups of four to read a part from the poem.

- Distribute copies of page 122.

- Have students use the script to practice and perform "Toucan."

Comprehension

- Ask students, "What is a toucan?" Use a graphic organizer/semantic web with a circle in the center. Write *toucan* in the circle. Have students tell all they know about toucans. What do they look like? Where do they live? What do they eat? Write students' responses on the graphic organizer.

- Tell students to use the information inside the graphic organizer to write about toucans.

Word Study Extension

Use page 123 to extend word concepts from the poem.

Toucan

Who can, who can,
Who can catch a toucan?
Lou can, Lou can,
Lou can catch a toucan.
Jan can, Jan can,
Jan can catch a toucan.
Sue can, Sue can,
Sue can catch a toucan.
One can, two can,
Three can catch a toucan.
Lou can, and Sue can,
Jan can catch a toucan.

—Tim Rasinski

Name: _____

Reader's Theater

Directions: In groups of four, select a part from the script. Practice reading your part with expression. Join with the other readers and practice the poem together. Perform for your class.

Toucan

Reader 1: Who can, who can, who can catch a toucan?

Reader 2: Lou can, Lou can, Lou can catch a toucan.

Reader 3: Jan can, Jan can, Jan can catch a toucan.

Reader 4: Sue can, Sue can, Sue can catch a toucan.

Reader 2: One can, two can, three can catch a toucan.

Reader 1: Lou can, and Sue can, Jan can catch a toucan.

Name: _____

Word Building

I. Directions: *Write words from the poem in the correct groups. Then add new words to each group.*

Words with -*an*	Words with -*ee*	Words with -*tch*	Words About Birds

II. Directions: *Read each sentence. Write the missing word. Use the Word Bank for help.*

1. *I slipped on a* _____ *and fell.*

2. *I saw* _____ *toucans at the zoo.*

3. *Mom made a* _____ *of cookies.*

4. *Our dog likes to* _____ *sticks.*

Word Bank

fetch   three
banana   batch

Clickity-Clack

See pages 10–11 for ideas to introduce the poem. Complete some or all of the following activities throughout the week. The activities on this page may be completed before, during, or after reading the poem. Select activities based on your students' needs.

Phonemic Awareness

- Tell students that you are going to say three words. They are to tell you the word that doesn't belong or sounds different from the other words.

- Say the words *pain*, *pail*, and *care*. Students should identify that *care* doesn't belong because it does not begin with the /p/ sound.

- Continue with the words listed below:

  stack, track, rain—*rain* doesn't belong

  sun, train, stop—*train* doesn't belong

  in, play, run—*play* doesn't belong

Phonics

- Write the word *clickity* on the board or on a sheet of chart paper. Underline the letters *cl* and tell students to substitute the letters *st* in place of the underlined letters. Students should respond with the nonsense word *stickity*.

- Distribute copies of page 126.

- Have students use the blends in the sentences to make silly words.

Vocabulary

- Explain to students that the prefix *re*- means "again" or "back." In the poem, the train goes into town, around and back.

- Write the following words on the board: *review, revisit,* and *rejoin*. Read the words one at a time and ask students if they think *re*- means "again" or "back" in each word.

Fluency

- Divide the class in half (boys/girls or down the middle of the room). Read the poem two lines at a time, with the two halves alternating reading each pair of lines. When students read, they should stand and then quickly sit when they are finished.

- Read the poem several times at different speeds. Students will enjoy the back-and-forth and up-and-down action of this activity.

Comprehension

- Explain that the author uses figurative language when describing the train. Read, "Blowing smoke from its stack as if it were in pain." Was the train in pain? What did the author mean by this phrase? What kind of a train is the author writing about?

- Tell students to use words from the poem to draw a picture of the train.

Word Study Extension

Use page 127 to extend word concepts from the poem.

Clickity-Clack

Clickity-clack down the track

Goes the choo-choo train,

Blowing smoke from its stack

As if it were in pain.

Clickity-clack down the track

Goes the choo-choo train,

Into town, around and back,

In sunshine and in rain.

—Tim Rasinski

Name: _____

Silly Sounds

Directions: In the poem, the train goes clickity-clack down the track. Make new sounds for the train by writing the underlined letters in each sentence in the blank spaces.

1. The train <u>sl</u>owly went down the track,

_____ ickity _____ ack.

2. The train <u>sh</u>ook down the track,

_____ ickity _____ ack.

3. The train <u>tr</u>aveled down the track,

_____ ickity _____ ack.

4. The train <u>ch</u>ugged down the track,

_____ ickity _____ ack.

5. The train <u>pl</u>owed down the track,

_____ ickity _____ ack.

6. The train <u>br</u>oke down on the track,

_____ ickity _____ ack.

7. The train <u>cr</u>eaked down the track,

_____ ickity _____ ack.

8. The train <u>wh</u>izzed down the track,

_____ ickity _____ ack.

Name: _____

Word Building

I. Directions: *Write words from the poem in the correct groups. Then add new words to each group.*

Words with *-ack*	Words with *-ick*	Words with *-ain*	Words About Trains

II. Directions: *Read each sentence. Write the missing word. Use the Word Bank for help.*

1. A computer _____ damaged our computer.

2. I am _____ to be a basketball player.

3. My brother is a _____ eater.

4. The grape jelly made a _____ on my new shirt.

Word Bank

training   stain
hacker   picky

A Real Pain

See pages 10–11 for ideas to introduce the poem. Complete some or all of the following activities throughout the week. The activities on this page may be completed before, during, or after reading the poem. Select activities based on your students' needs.

Phonemic Awareness

- Tell students that you will say a word and then ask them to substitute a sound in the word to make a new word. Say *pain*. Have students change the /p/ in *pain* to /r/ (*rain*).

- Practice with the words listed below:

  Change the /t/ in *town* to /d/—*down*

  Change the /b/ in *back* to /p/—*pack*

  Change the /d/ in *paid* to /l/—*pail*

Phonics

- Ask students to create a word family by adding letters to the beginning of the rime *-eal*. Tell students to add the /r/ sound to *-eal* (*real*).

- Continue with the following sounds below:

  Add /d/ to *-eal* (*deal*)

  Add /h/ to *-eal* (*heal*)

  Add /m/ to *-eal* (*meal*)

  Add /s/ to *-eal* (*seal*)

Vocabulary

- Tell students that words that sound the same but are spelled differently and have different meanings are called *homophones*. Write the words *ant* and *aunt* on the board or on a sheet of chart paper. Ask students to explain the meaning of each word. Record students' responses.

- Distribute copies of page 130.

- Tell students they will select the correct homophone to complete each sentence.

Fluency

- Have students use a red crayon to circle the rhyming words in the poem. These words will help with the phrasing of this poem.

- Have students use a blue crayon to underline three interesting or unusual words in the poem.

- Have students work in pairs to discuss their underlined words and practice choral reading or reading in silly voices.

Comprehension

- Ask students to fold a blank sheet of paper to make four boxes. Have students number the boxes 1–4.

- Reread the poem. Ask students to sequence the events in the poem in order and to write and illustrate a sentence to describe each event.

Word Study Extension

Use page 131 to extend word concepts from the poem.

A Real Pain

My sister's a real big pain.

I think she's driving me insane.

She stays in the bathroom

For hours at a time,

And when she comes out,

Her hair's full of slime!

She's on the phone

Twenty hours a day,

And when she hangs up,

She thinks of more to say.

My sister's a real big pain.

I think she's driving me insane.

—Tim Rasinski

Name: _____

Homophones

Directions: Homophones are words that sound the same but are spelled differently and have different meanings. Read each sentence. Choose the correct word to complete the sentence.

their *there*	**1.** Malia left her coat over _____.
hear *here*	**2.** I _____ my mom calling me for dinner.
pane *pain*	**3.** I ate so much that my stomach is in _____.
sun *son*	**4.** Ali played soccer in the hot _____.
Its *It's*	**5.** _____ fun to have a picnic with my family.
eight *ate*	**6.** My brother goes to bed at _____ o'clock.
two *too*	**7.** I want to go, _____.
know *no*	**8.** I _____ the answer to the question.
write *right*	**9.** Follow the rules and make the _____ choices.
see *sea*	**10.** The ship is traveling across the _____.

Challenge: Find three more sets of homophones. Draw a picture to illustrate each word.

Name: _____

Word Building

I. Directions: *Write words from the poem in the correct groups. Then add new words to each group.*

Words with -*one*	Words with -*ain*	Words with -*ane*	Words About Siblings

II. Directions: *Read each sentence. Write the missing word. Use the Word Bank for help.*

1. The dog next door is a Great _____.

2. The ice cream _____ melted in a minute.

3. The horse's _____ was brushed and trimmed.

4. It is _____ to write with a broken hand.

Word Bank

cone   *painful*   Dane   mane

Flying

See pages 10–11 for ideas to introduce the poem. Complete some or all of the following activities throughout the week. The activities on this page may be completed before, during, or after reading the poem. Select activities based on your students' needs.

Phonemic Awareness

- Tell students that you are going to say three words. They are to tell you which sound the words have in common.

- Say the words *plane*, *pet*, and *play*. Students should identify the /p/ sound as the sound the words have in common.

- Continue with the words below:

  fly, friend, four—beginning /f/ sound

  helicopter, hot, hair—beginning /h/ sound

  balloon, moon, down—ending /n/ sound

  start, soon, sun—beginning /s/ sound

  come, swim, ram—ending /m/ sound

Phonics

- Tell students to make new words by selecting random letters to add to the beginning of the rime *-oon*. Explain that many of the new words will be nonsense words.

- Challenge students to categorize the words as real or nonsense as they verbally go through the alphabet. Help students get started by modeling the following:

  aoon   *boon*   *coon*

  doon   *eoon*   *foon*

Vocabulary

- Write the words *flying machines* on the board or on a sheet of chart paper. Have students brainstorm other flying machines. Record their responses.

- Ask students to circle flying machine words mentioned in the poem and write the purpose of each flying machine (e.g., *jet plane*—to carry people; *helicopter*—for the police to help people; *hot air balloon*—to take people for a ride).

Fluency

- Explain that the author has placed punctuation in this poem for proper phrasing. Be sure to draw students' attention to the commas and periods. Read the poem aloud.

- Ask students to select one line from the poem and write it in large print on a sheet of paper or a sentence strip. Reread the poem and have students stand to read their lines.

Comprehension

- Play "What is it?" with students by giving clues about a word from the poem.

- Say clues one at a time to reveal information about the selected vocabulary word. For example, with the word *helicopter*, you can say it zooms through the sky, if someone is hurt it can take them to the hospital quickly.

- Distribute copies of page 134.

- Tell students they will read the story clues to answer the questions.

Word Study Extension

Use page 135 to extend word concepts from the poem.

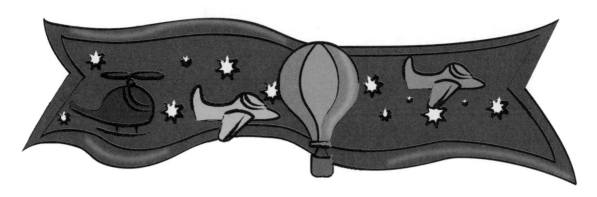

Flying

Helicopter, jet planes,

Hot air balloon.

I want to fly,

Fly really soon.

I'm flying today,

Starting at noon.

By ten o'clock,

I'll be circling the moon!

—Tim Rasinski

Name: _____

Flying Machines

Directions: Read each clue and answer the questions below in complete sentences. Use the words from the Word Bank to help you.

1. Danny was playing in the park when he saw something in the sky. It was large and round. It had a basket on the bottom and people waved at him. What was it?

    _____

2. Danny watched as it floated by. Suddenly, he saw something else high in the sky. It had two wings and a tail. It was moving quickly and its engine made a loud noise. What was it?

    _____

3. Danny watched as it zoomed across the sky. Danny heard another sound in the sky. He saw a large propeller on the top of the machine. It was flying slowly and Danny could see the word "Rescue" on its side. What was it?

    _____

4. Danny started to walk home. He saw something else in the sky. It was small with wings and a tail. It flapped its wings and landed on a tree branch. What was it?

    _____

Word Bank

   jet   hot air balloon   bird   helicopter

• •

Challenge: On a separate sheet of paper, write a story about an adventure on an unusual flying machine.

Name: _____

Word Building

I. Directions: *Write words from the poem in the correct groups. Then add new words to each group.*

Words with *-oon*	Words with *-ock*	Words with *-ing*	Words About Airplanes

• •

II. Directions: *Read each sentence. Write the missing word. Use the Word Bank for help.*

1. *Lunch is at _____ today.*

2. *The rocket was _____ faster than sound.*

3. *The _____ fell off his horse near the finish line.*

4. *Hot air _____ fly peacefully through the sky.*

Word Bank

flying   balloons   noontime   jockey

Answer Key

Page 18
1. top
2. dog
3. log
4. pot
5. sock

Page 19
Students' answers may vary. Sample answers are provided below.

Words with -one
alone   phone
bone   cone, stone

Words with -ome
home   dome
Rome

Words with -ice
ice   rice
mice   lice

Words About Being Alone
quiet   single
fun   lonely
1. phone
2. bones
3. home
4. nice

Page 22
Students should've circled *think* and *drink* with a blue crayon, and *drain* and *rain* with a red crayon.

Page 23
Students' answers may vary. Sample answers are provided below.

Words with -ink
think   drink
stink   link

Words with -ain
drain   rain
brain   gain

Words with -et
get   let
met   set

Words About Rain
wet   drops
water   drizzle
1. sink
2. get
3. rain
4. drink

Page 26
Students' answers will vary.

Page 27
Students' answers may vary. Sample answers are provided below.

Words with -ark
park   dark
bark   stark

Words with -ide
ride   slide
glide   hide

Words with -oot
scooter   hoot
boot   root

Words About Scooters
wheels   fast
scoot   fun
1. hide
2. dark
3. hoot
4. slide

Page 31
Students' answers may vary. Sample answers are provided below.

Words with -un
Uncle   run
sun   stun   fun

Words with -ope
mope   rope
hope   dope

Words with -ike
bike   Mike
hike   like

Words About Exercise
sweat   work
energy   healthy
1. sun
2. hope
3. bike
4. mope

Page 34
1. plow
2. bow
3. tow
4. now
5. grow
6. cow

Page 35
Students' answers may vary. Sample answers are provided below.

Words with -ent
went   tent
twenty   bent   sent

Words with -own
downtown   clowns
frown   down

Words with -oo
oops   look
took   shook

Words About the Circus
clowns   tents
rings   acrobats
1. town
2. dent
3. hook
4. sent

Page 38
Happy Halloween
Creepy crying cats
Big black bats
Jagged-jawed jack-o' lanterns
Terrible twins trick or treat
Kids collecting candy
Happy Halloween

Answer Key (cont.)

Page 39

Students' answers may vary. Sample answers are provided below.

Words with -een

seen   Halloween
teen   spleen

Words with -er

spider   cider
her   singer

Words with -ack

black   tack
back   shack

Words About Halloween

witches   costumes
candy   ghosts

1. teenager
2. queen
3. cider
4. stack

Page 42

1. The little boy is green.
2. He is from Mars.
3. He asked if he could come out to play.
4. They flew in his spaceship to the Milky Way.
5. Students' answers will vary.
6. Students' answers will vary.

Page 43

Students' answers may vary. Sample answers are provided below.

Words with -ay

day   play
away   way   stay

Words with -oy

boy   toy
joy   Roy

Words with -out

out   throughout
shout   spout   pout

Words About Outer Space

stars   planets
asteroids   rockets

1. shout
2. Roy, Floyd
3. pout
4. day

Page 46

People—clowns, trapeze artist, lion-tamer, acrobat, tightrope walker

Animals—tigers, elephants, monkeys, ponies, bears

Page 47

Students' answers may vary. Sample answers are provided below.

Words with -own

town   brown
clown   gown

Words with -ame

came   same
tame   shame

Words with -us

circus   bus
Gus

Words About Clowns

wig   costume
tricks   silly

1. plus
2. tame
3. town
4. down

Page 50

1. qu
2. ch
3. sh
4. ch
5. sh
6. qu
7. th
8. th
9. sh
10. ch
11. qu
12. ch
13. th
14. sh
15. th
16. qu

Page 51

Students' answers may vary. Sample answers are provided below.

Words with -ay

day   way
say   stay

Words with -ant

ants   pant
Santa   antler

Words with -ight

fight   right
light   night

Words About Friends

friendly   nice
pals   kind

1. stay
2. antlers
3. right
4. pants

Page 54

Students' answers may vary. Sample answers are provided below.

-op—shop, mop, pop, chop, stop, slop, hop, clop

-out—shout, pout, stout, clout

Students' sentences will vary. Sample sentences are provided below.

1. I like to grocery shop with my mom.
2. I pout when I have to clean my room.

Answer Key *(cont.)*

Page 55

Students' answers will vary. Sample answers are provided below.

Words with -op

pop   stop

shop   cop

Words with -ime

lime   time

dime   mime

Words with -ver

never   ever

fever

Words About Soda

bubbles   fizz

cool   refreshing

1. silver
2. dime
3. flopped
4. slime

Page 58

Accept appropriate answers. Students' answers will vary. Sample answers are provided below.

1. We can skate on the pond when it freezes.
2. My cap keeps my head warm.
3. It is cold in the winter.

Page 59

Students' answers may vary. Sample answers are provided below.

Words with -ow

blow   snow

low   know

Words with -ice

ice   rice

dice   nice

Words with -im

dim   Tim

swim   him

Words About Fish

scales   slimy

wet   worms

1. slice
2. rice
3. know
4. Tim

Page 62

Dear (name),

Please come to my **birthday** party. We will play **games** like musical chairs. We will eat **cake** and **ice cream**. Chocolate is my favorite. After you sing **happy** birthday to me, I will **blow** out the candles. Then I can open my **presents**. We will have lots of **fun**.

Sincerely,

(name)

Page 63

Students' answers may vary. Sample answers are provided below.

Words with -ake

cake   shake

take   make

Words with -ee

see   tree

fee   bee

Words with -air

chairs   hair

stair   fair

Words About Birthdays

candles   cake

games   party

1. wake
2. tree
3. chair
4. snowflakes

Page 66

Students' answers may vary. Sample answers are provided below.

st—still, steal, straw, step, start, sting, steep, sty, stash, stall

sm—smite, smart, smug, small, smash

sw—sweat, swim, sweet, swill, swing, sweep

wh—whim, white, wheat, where, when, why

Page 67

Students' answers may vary. Sample answers are provided below.

Words with -eet

feet   sheet

meet   beet   greet

Words with -ell

smelly   smell

tell   shell   fell

Words with -ill

still   Bill

dill   mill

Words About Smelly Feet

stinky   socks

sweaty   phew

1. sheets
2. dill
3. tells
4. fleet

Page 70

1. ringing
2. singing
3. talking
4. squawking
5. pressing
6. telling
7. singing
8. pressing
9. ringing
10. squawking
11. talking
12. telling

Page 71

Students' answers may vary. Sample answers are provided below.

Words with -inger

singer   ringer
finger   linger

Words with -alk

talk   walk
stalk

Words with -ess

press   dress
guess   mess

Words About Telephones

ringer   numbers
talk   call

1. guess
2. stalk
3. stinger
4. finger

Page 74

Across

3. sweet
5. feel

Down

1. bee
2. steel
3. seed
4. tree
5. feed

Page 75

Students' answers may vary. Sample answers are provided below.

Words with -ike

like   bike
Mike   hike

Words with -eed

seed   tweed
deed   greed

Words with -eet

sweet   beet
feet   meet

Words That Rhyme

tree   bee
see   me

1. sleet
2. deed
3. hike
4. bike

Page 78

1. duck
2. sheep
3. pig
4. hen
5. horse
6. cow
7. dog
8. rabbit

Page 79

Students' answers may vary. Sample answers are provided below.

Words with -eep

sheep   sleep
keep   deep

Words with -ings

ducklings   wings
sings   kings

Words with -ick

chicks   kick
lick   stick

Words About Animals

horses   sheep
duckling   chicks

1. sheep
2. chickens
3. wings
4. steep

Page 82

1. up
2. light
3. happy
4. buy
5. right
6. thin
7. first
8. strong
9. push

Page 83

Students' answers may vary. Sample answers are provided below.

Words with -ast

last   blast
fast   cast

Words with -out

shout   out
pout

Words with -ull

full   gull
dull   hull

Words that are Opposites

top   bottom
full   empty

1. trout
2. full
3. blasted
4. pulled

Page 86

1. i
2. o
3. e
4. a
5. a
6. u
7. i
8. o
9. u
10. e
11. o
12. u

Answer Key (cont.)

Page 87

Students' answers may vary. Sample answers are provided below.

Word with -at

cat brat
sat splat

Words with -og

hog dog
log smog

Words with -up

up puppy
cup

Words About Growing Up

tall mature
adult big

1. bogged
2. guppy
3. rattle
4. runners

Page 90

Things I Need—sleep, bed, blanket, teddy bear, pajamas, slippers, pillow, bath, toothbrush
Things I Do—sleep, good-night kiss, bathe
Places I Sleep—bedroom, bed, parents' room, couch
Students' sentences will vary.

Page 91

Students' answers may vary. Sample answers are provided below.

Words with -orn

worn torn
born horn

Words with -end

end bend
tend send

Words with -ing

thing rings
king sting bring

Words About Old Things

worn dull
special antiques

1. friends
2. born
3. tingle
4. corner

Page 94

1. tree
2. bear
3. rabbit
4. ball
5. candy
6. car
7. sweet, chewy
8. soft, furry
9. round, bouncy
10. fast, shiny
11. scary/brown; tall/green

Page 95

Students' answers may vary. Sample answers are provided below.

Words with -ape

grapes shapes
cape tape

Words with -um

plums tummy
yum sum

Words with -each

peaches each
teach beach

Words About Fruit

apples sweet
yummy healthy

1. beach
2. cape
3. pump
4. Each

Page 99

Students' answers may vary. Sample answers are provided below.

Words with -oop

coop scoop
hoop loop

Words with -ish

radish dish
fish wish

Words with -ake

make take
stake lake

Words About Farm Animals

horses chickens
cows sheep

1. dishes
2. coop
3. stakes
4. radishes

Page 102

1. It was inside my tent.
2. The crickets and the bird were singing.
3. It was night.
4. Twinkling stars and the moon were in the sky.
5. It was crackling.
6. It was summer.
7. Yes, it is her favorite thing.
8. Students' answers will vary.

Page 103
Students' answers may vary. Sample answers are provided below.
Words with *-ong*
song   long
dong   Ping-Pong
Words with *-oon*
moon   soon
baboon   spoon
Words with *-une*
tune   June
dune
Words About Camping
tent   hiking
fire   sleeping bag
  1. croon
  2. *King Kong*
  3. June
  4. moonlight

Page 106
  1. flock
  2. proof
  3. scan
  4. spot
  5. crock
  6. slid
  7. men, met
  8. pain, pail
  9. sick, sock
  10. pour, pout

Page 107
Students' answers may vary. Sample answers are provided below.
Words with *-ock*
flock   sock
tock   dock
Words with *-out*
scout   out
shout   pout
Words with *-en*
ten   hen
Ben   den
Words About Numbers
ten   zero
five   counting
  1. scouts
  2. lock
  3. when
  4. shocked

Page 111
Students' answers may vary. Sample answers are provided below.
Words with *-ike*
like   hike
bike   Mike
Words with *-oop*
hoop   loop
coop   troop
Words with *-oup*
group   soup
Words About Sports
game   teams
champion   competition
  1. soup
  2. whoops
  3. like
  4. coop

Page 114
  1. kite
  2. cane
  3. hide
  4. tape
  5. plane
  6. plane/kite
  7. hide
  8. cane
  9. tape
  10. kite/plane

Page 115
Students' answers may vary. Sample answers are provided below.
Words with *-op*
pop   drop
hop   bop
shop
Words with *-ole*
whole   stole
hole   mole
Words with *-ink*
drink   sink
stink   rink
Words About My Favorite Drink
fizzy   cold
refreshing   canned
  1. pop
  2. stink
  3. hole
  4. stole

Page 118
Students' answers will vary. Sample lost pet poster shown below.
Lost **Dog**
Please help me find **Max**!
He is a large black Lab.
He is wearing a collar with his name on it.
If found, **please call (555)555-5555.**

Answer Key (cont.)

Page 119

Students' answers may vary. Sample answers are provided below.

Words with -ill

pill   ill
still   fill

Words with -et

pet   vet
set   net

Words with -ot

cot   rot
knot   shot

Words About Being Sick

ill   fever
tired   bed

1. got
2. kettle
3. chills
4. setting

Page 122

Students should read the poem with expression.

Page 123

Students' answers may vary. Sample answers are provided below.

Words with -an

can   toucan
tan   man

Words with -ee

three   bee
see   knee

Words with -tch

catch   match
patch   latch

Words About Birds

toucan   squawk
beak   feathers

1. banana
2. three
3. batch
4. fetch

Page 126

1. slickity slack
2. shickity shack
3. trickity track
4. chickity chack
5. plickity plack
6. brickity brack
7. crikity crack
8. whickity whack

Page 127

Students' answers may vary. Sample answers are provided below.

Words with -ack

track   stack
back   tack

Words with -ick

clickity   tick
sick   lick

Words with -ain

train   rain
stain   drain

Words About Trains

choo choo   track
smoke   long

1. hacker
2. training
3. picky
4. stain

Page 130

1. there
2. hear
3. pain
4. sun
5. It's
6. eight
7. too
8. know
9. right
10. sea

Page 131

Students' answers may vary. Sample answers are provided below.

Words with -one

phone   tone
cone   stone

Words with -ain

pain   rain
train   drain

Words with -ane

insane   pane
plane   crane

Words About Siblings

brother   sister
friends   enemies

1. Dane
2. cone
3. mane
4. painful

Page 134

1. It was a hot air balloon.
2. It was a jet airplane.
3. It was a helicopter.
4. It was a bird.

Page 135

Students' answers may vary. Sample answers are provided below.

Words with -oon

soon   noon
moon   spoon

Words with -ock

o'clock   tock
shock   smock

Words with -ing

circling   king
bring   sting

Words About Airplanes

wings   fast
airports   pilot

1. noontime
2. flying
3. jockey
4. balloons

References Cited

Adams, M. J. 1990. *Beginning to read: Thinking and learning about print.* Cambridge, MA: MIT Press.

Baker, S., D. C. Simmons, and E.J. Kameenui. Eds. 1998. *What reading research tells us about children with diverse learning needs: Basses and basics.* Mahwah, NJ: Erlbaum.

Ball, E. W., and B.A. Blachman. 1991. Does phoneme segmentation training in kindergarten make a difference in early word recognition and developmental spelling? *Reading Research Quarterly* 26:49–86.

Bottomley, D. and J. Osborn. 1993. *Implementing reciprocal teaching with fourth and fifth grade Students in content area reading.* ERIC Document 361668.

Bromage, B. K., and R. E. Mayer. 1986. Quantitative and qualitative effects of repetition on learning from technical text. *Journal of Educational Psychology* 78:271–278.

Carter, C. 1997. Why reciprocal teaching? *Educational Leadership* 54:64–68.

Fry, E. 1998. The most common phonograms. *The Reading Teacher* 51:620–622.

Gaskins, I., L. Ehri, C. Cress, C. O'Hara, and K. Donnelly. 1996/1997. Procedures for word learning: Making discoveries about words. *The Reading Teacher* 50:312–328.

Herrell, A., and M. Jordan. 2004. *Fifty strategies for teaching English language learners.* 2nd ed. Upper Saddle, NJ: Pearson Education, Inc.

Hosenfeld, C. 1993. *Activities and materials for implementing adapted versions of reciprocal teaching in beginning, intermediate, and advanced levels of instruction in English, Spanish, and French as a second/foreign language.* ERIC Document ED370354.

Jensen, E. 1998. *Teaching with the brain in mind.* Alexandria, VA: Association for Supervision and Curriculum Development.

LaBerge, D., and S. J. Samuels. 1974. Toward a theory of automatic information processing in reading. *Cognitive Psychology* 5:293–323.

National Reading Panel. 2000. *Teaching children to read: An evidence-based assessment of the scientific research literature on reading and its implications for reading instruction.* Report of the National Reading Panel. Washington, DC: U.S. Government Print Office.

O'Shea, L. J., and P. T. Sindelar. 1983. The effects of segmenting written discourse on reading comprehension of low-and high-performance readers. *Reading Research Quarterly* 18:458–465.

Pressley, M. 2002. *Comprehension instruction: What makes sense now, what might make sense soon.* ERIC Document EJ667632.

Rasinski, T. V. 2003. *The Fluent Reader.* New York: Scholastic Professional Books.

Rosenshine, B. and C. Meister. 1994. Reciprocal teaching: A review of the research. *Review of Educational Research* 64:479–530.

Samuels, S. J. 1979. The method of repeated reading. *The Reading Teacher* 32:403–408.

Stanovich, K. E. 1986. Matthew effects in reading: Some consequences of individual differences in the acquisition of literacy. *Reading Research Quarterly* 21:360–407.

WIDA—housed within the Wisconsin Center for Education Research. 2007. English language proficiency standards. The Board of Regents of the University of Wisconsin System, http://www.wida.us/standards/elp.aspx

Yopp, H. K. 1988. The validity and reliability of phonemic awareness tests. *Reading Research Quarterly* 23:159–177.

Yopp, H. K. 1992. Developing phonemic awareness in young children. *The Reading Teacher* 45:696–704.

Contents of the CDs

Contents of the Teacher Resource CD

Poems and Activity Pages		
Lesson	**Pages**	**Filename**
1	17–19	lesson1.pdf
2	21–23	lesson2.pdf
3	25–27	lesson3.pdf
4	29–31	lesson4.pdf
5	33–35	lesson5.pdf
6	37–39	lesson6.pdf
7	41–43	lesson7.pdf
8	45–47	lesson8.pdf
9	49–51	lesson9.pdf
10	53–55	lesson10.pdf
11	57–59	lesson11.pdf
12	61–63	lesson12.pdf
13	65–67	lesson13.pdf
14	69–71	lesson14.pdf
15	73–75	lesson15.pdf
16	77–79	lesson16.pdf
17	81–83	lesson17.pdf
18	85–87	lesson18.pdf
19	89–91	lesson19.pdf
20	93–95	lesson20.pdf
21	97–99	lesson21.pdf
22	101–103	lesson22.pdf
23	105–107	lesson23.pdf
24	109–111	lesson24.pdf
25	113–115	lesson25.pdf
26	117–119	lesson26.pdf
27	121–123	lesson27.pdf
28	125–127	lesson28.pdf
29	129–131	lesson29.pdf
30	133–135	lesson30.pdf

Additional Resources	
Item	**Filename**
Page-turning Book	level3.html
Instructional Plan	instructional.pdf
McREL Chart	mcrelchart.pdf
Activity Skill Corr. Chart	activitychart.pdf

Contents of the Audio CD

Track	Title
01	Home Alone
02	The Drain
03	My Scooter
04	Exercise
05	Twenty-Two Lions
06	Hallowen
07	A Little Green Boy
08	The Circus
09	Ants
10	Soda Pop
11	The Wind Will Blow
12	Happy Birthday to Me
13	Smelly Feet
14	My Telephone
15	Alphabet Rhyme
16	Number Rhyme
17	Opposites
18	Growing Up
19	My Blanket
20	Yum Yum
21	Animal Stew
22	Camping
23	Ten
24	Hula-Hoop
25	Grape Pop
26	Sick Pet
27	Toucan
28	Clickity-Clack
29	A Real Pain
30	Flying